IF I'D KNOWN THEN

WHAT I KNOW NOW

The High Cost of Spiritual Confusion

Donna Ferguson

THE
LESSTRANG
GROUP

Palm Desert, California

© 2000 Donna Ferguson, Newport Beach, CA 92660   All rights reserved
P.O. Box 15951
Newport Beach, CA 92659
e-mail: noneutralground@aol.com

ISBN 1-0887449-08-6

Designed by Kathleen Thorne-Thomsen

Manufactured in the United States of America

ACKNOWLEDGMENTS

Often those who stand behind the one who gets the credit are known only to God and each other. This is one of those times. Fifteen years ago, God began to build the team that would make this book a reality. It was God who gave the vision and charted its course from the beginning. To each of you who has traveled with me in the completion of this work, my deepest love and appreciation for your commitment to God and to me. It is my earnest prayer that we see the fruit of our journey in the lives of those for whom it was undertaken.

DEDICATION

To my Lord and Savior, Jesus Christ
in gratitude and awe for all He has done

Table of Contents

✠

Introduction

We've heard all our lives that what we don't know won't hurt us and too many of us believed it. It's what we don't know that can hurt us the most when it comes to our understanding of God. And a little knowledge can be as dangerous as no knowledge at all when we are influenced by those as spiritually confused as ourselves. This is what makes us disciples of our own opinions rather than disciples of Christ.

What we believe becomes the truth we are going to live by; even when what we profess as truth is founded on deception. As the natural and the supernatural worlds compete for our attention and the ultimate destiny of our souls, we are thrust into the crossfire of a righteous God and Satanic forces—both powers operating from an eternal perspective—which is both the heartbeat and the drumbeat of this book.

There is an eternal outcome to every aspect of our lives; therefore, it is imperative that as women we cultivate this perspective, particularly in those areas which undermine our relationships with God, our families, and our role as coexecutors of His will within these relationships.

All things are not going to work together for the good of those who remain indifferent to God. Yes, His love is unconditional. His promises are not! The Christian life is a serious and holy occupation—a courageous and at times consuming endeavor—and if we belong to Christ we will learn, one way or another, that it is better to be trained by divine love than indulgence.

The day is coming when we will present the fruit of our lives before the King of Kings. This harvest will depend on how willing we are to prepare for and then engage in the tilling, planting, and tending of the particular soil given us for this purpose. But before we can serve God, we must learn to serve each other. It is in the tending to the family plot that our first fruits are produced; from these first fruits we are then equipped to work in other fields of His choosing. Those who remain single will have opportunities compatible with their circumstances, as God redirects their longings into the stream of His compassion to meet a need elsewhere.

When my children were growing up I said, "You'll be an adult a lot longer than you'll be a child, so listen up. I'm trying to prepare you for life." Knowing what I know now I say, "Your time on earth is limited; eternity is forever, so pay attention." When we consider that our lives will be tested as to how we used our talents, resources, and the very number of days allotted to us, it behooves us to find out what God has to say to us in this regard.

This is not a book to help us feel better about ourselves, but to move us beyond ourselves, that we might respond to the call of Christ without reservation or complaint. It is further intended to encourage those who are picking up the pieces of what has already transpired in their lives, to mentor the young, and to inspire those who have crossed the threshold of middle age.

As women we cannot pass on to our daughters what we do not first harbor within ourselves, and after 10 years of involvement with broken women I know their need. It was this same need that drove my mother to suicide and claimed two-thirds of my life.

Being female is a lot more complicated than we ever anticipated when we were growing up, and by the time we come to any understanding of what it's all about, most of us have reached a considerable age, and our children are off repeating our mistakes. For the most part we hide our fears from our daughters, paint a picture of marriage and motherhood the way we would like them to turn out, then try to console them when they stumble over the same unreasonable expectations we tripped over.

We are not lining up to admit our inability to make a better go of our lives. Who wants to admit to failure? Who wants to confess that they have fallen short of what they set out to be and what God created us to be? Yet if we who are older are going to teach the young, we must be willing to admit to our mistakes, for without honesty we have nothing of substance to offer.

The heart cry of women today is what it has always been. As little girls we look first to our fathers, then to our boyfriends, and finally to our husbands to meet an inborn need to be cherished, a need divinely woven into our character and as much a part of our make up as the physical traits that identify us as female. When the men in our lives are not able or willing to cherish—that is to value, respect, appreciate, and consider us—our identity and value as a person is threatened. This is where many of us make the mistake of allowing the men we love to become our gods. If anyone other than the Lord of Heaven holds that position in our lives we will be ruled by the attitudes of others and become less responsive to God.

There is a strength and perspective that comes with the struggle for wholeness. Women need these models of encouragement. When I suggest myself as such a model it is because I can boast only in Jesus Christ Who gave me what I could never have gained on my own. It is the fallen, when standing again, that can best encourage the fallen, and the revived heart that best understands the sick-at-heart. Yet without honesty, any effort on my part to encourage others will fail, and I begin by saying, up front, that mending the breaches of our lives requires a particular type of courage and perseverance available only through the nurturing of the Holy Spirit.

We need to see this evidence in the lives of others before we can believe that we can make it too. But believing we can make it is entirely different than believing in ourselves. When the self is damaged we don't have the emotional components within ourselves to build on—and we know it—so to believe in ourselves doesn't work anymore than whistling in the dark will make us any less afraid of the dark. Our most desperate need is knowledge of God and then to apply what we learn about God into life *with* God.

We are the sum total of our experience from infancy on, and when these experiences have been damaging, the outcome is ours to change. We *can* look forward to a satisfying conclusion to our lives. The question is: are we willing to trust a God who did not alter these circumstances in the first place? Isaiah 53:11, in speaking of our Lord, tells us that He would look upon the fruit of the travail of His soul and be satisfied. God, in the Person of Jesus Christ, invested His suffering on our behalf that we might become the fruit of His life. When we attempt to bypass the pain of revising the outcome of our lives, we risk the eternal fruit of our souls and the treasure God has for us.

We cannot run people through a pain detector, give them a dose of hurt-no-more scriptures, then expect them to forget where they've been and what happened to them while they were there. Emotional healing is a process, and within this process a separate and even greater process is taking place: the conforming work of Romans 8:29.

It is in the restructuring of our wounds that our losses and disappointments become the raw materials with which God builds what might not otherwise be built. Only when we have turned this corner in our understanding can we appreciate the potential of our difficult seasons, and be equipped to partner with God in what He longs to do through those difficulties.

My credentials are those of experience and victory, the fruit of a long and trying spiritual pursuit which included much speculation over the grand scheme of things, and years of prayer and study. I admit that many of my wilderness years were of my own making, the outcome of ignorance and foolish choices, but out of them has come a field in which to co-labor with Christ, and fruit for the travail of my soul.

How sweet it is to come to a place in life where you can accept the person you turned out to be; when the grand scheme of things finally makes sense; and the things that really matter—really *do* matter. Still I cannot help but wonder where I might be today, where my family might be today, had I known 30 years ago what I know now.

If only I'd known:

There is no neutral ground in the universe.
Not all angels are interested in our welfare.
We can't judge God's love by our circumstances.
We don't have to accept the price others put on us.
A half truth is still a lie.
Assumptions can be deadly.
Perfectionism is not a virtue but a disease.
How easy it is to fall in need and mistake it for love.
It takes more than time to heal a broken heart.
What we see is not always what we get.
Life is a school to prepare us for eternity.
We don't have to go to seminary to understand the Bible.

Did I have to learn everything the hard way?

Do you?

I

It's My Life ... Isn't It?

✠

When I reached the age of 21 I thought the world would make a place for me. Nobody could tell me what to do anymore. I could go where I wanted and do what I wanted. Things were going to be different now that I was in charge. By age 30 I realized that the world was not going to carve out a spot for me—I still wasn't getting my share of the pie—and I was as affected by the moods and behaviors of others as I'd always been. At 40 I was facing a health crisis, and every loss I'd endured thus far was standing between me and whatever time I had left, reminding me that I'd accomplished little of what I intended to do, and most of what I swore I'd never do.

Surely I wasn't going to have one of those typical midlife crises. Not after all I'd come through. I was too tough for that! Wasn't I? People always told me how strong I was. How could it be then, that after all these years, I found myself trapped in a panic as painful as the tracks of the surgeon's knife?

I've cried out to God when I wasn't sure He was even listening. I've prayed in anger through clenched teeth, and with tears of gratitude, but no prayer is more dear to me than the prayer I discovered in a painting on the wall at the foot of my hospital bed when I was 40. A small sailboat was caught in an ocean storm. These words were printed across the water:

Dear Lord help me!
The ocean is so wide and I have such a little boat.

For the first time in my life I felt that I was finally telling God what I'd always wanted to tell Him. My ocean was wide, *and* stormy. My boat could have capsized many times. And I wasn't sure that this time it wouldn't. The doctors advised me to get my affairs in order before I checked into the hospital, and could not guarantee that the surgery would prevent any further damage to my kidneys. There was Demerol for the physical pain, but nothing to dull the emotional distress assaulting me day and night. My physical condition was no longer my main concern. I was in a spiritual crisis, suffering from a lack of knowledge of God.

"What we think about God," wrote A. W. Tozer, "is the most important thing about us."[1] My thinking was flawed. And I could trace it back to another hospital stay that began the night my mother, Elizabeth, turned on the gas in our apartment, intending to take me and my little brother with her. When they broke down the door they found her sitting dead in the rocking chair, with the two of us unconscious at her feet.

Twelve years later, while in nurses' training, I found myself in the hospital a second time. It was the night of the school dance, and I had a date with a medical student named Charlie. I was determined not to miss the dance, in spite of the abdominal pain I'd suffered all week, but before I could get into my formal I collapsed and was rushed into surgery. The first voice I heard when I woke was that of the surgeon.

"You must have a special mission in life, young lady! You've cheated death twice tonight! First of all, we had to remove a foot of gangrenous intestine; the appendix had completely strangulated the bowel. I don't see how you managed to live, let alone stay on your feet all week, with a mess like that stewing inside you. And that's not all! An oil tanker ran a red light and slammed into Charlie's car right where you would have been sitting. If you'd kept your date with Charlie, you wouldn't be alive. It's a good thing you fainted when you did. The impact would have ruptured your intestines, even if you survived the crash itself. Either way, you'd be dead."

The surgeon didn't believe in coincidence, but credited my survival to the efforts of a diligent guardian angel who stepped in to avert the play of circumstances against my life. I wondered at the time what he might say if he knew I'd already cheated death the night my mother planned a family suicide? Would he say I had even more important things to do? He was still shaking his head days later over the timing of the events, given the consequences of a ruptured bowel. "If you'd been anywhere but on the operating table during that hour . . ."

Sometimes God uses the people we have the least to do with to impact us the most. We don't recognize His hand in it at the time, but looking back we see how He orchestrated the circumstances for our good. This man was the first to suggest I had a purpose. His words would revive me many times, most importantly during a period when I was dangerously swayed by the opinion that God was against me. But it was the surgeon's opinion—the more flattering opinion—that prevailed.

The doctor who saved my life also made it livable. Without the memory of our conversation to draw from, any number of things might have happened. And much of what *did* happen might never have taken place.

How tragic it is that so few of us catch the vision of what we are meant to be until the greater portion of our life is spent. The truth is that *each of us has something special to do with the gift of life.* What makes the doing of it possible is available to anyone willing to search for it.

> And search we must!
> For life is much more than the pursuit of happiness.
> Life has a far higher purpose than what's in it for us.
> Our lives are, first of all, a matter of what's in it for God.

God is not observing our individual human dramas like a spectator in a distant cosmic theater. He is with us every step of the way, and whether we are aware of it or not, intricately involved in all our affairs. However, if we are to live with God as we were created to do, we must be willing to fit into the plans He has for each of us. The gap between our will and His will begins to narrow once we understand that the purpose of life is to prepare us for eternity.

All of life is about eternity, and the part we are destined to play in the unfolding of that purpose—it's about going to heaven and taking as many people with us as we can—something I have been obsessed with since my mother's suicide.

What a Difference a Day Makes

The circumstances surrounding my birth mother's death were beyond the reasoning of a seven-year-old, so I buried the grief of living without her, but the feelings belonging to *her* death would resurface four years later when my adoptive mother, Beatrice, suffered a stroke.

I remember perching at the top of the staircase with my body pressed into the banister. Three days I perched, rising when the door opened, but the white hill on the bed never shifted. On the fourth day the priest came to the house and I was packed off to spend the night with family friends. The following morning a grim-faced woman sat down on the side of the bed and took my hand. I listened to what she said; watched the words, like machine-gun rounds, fire from her teeth. I was not going to cry. Beatrice was not dead. It was all a mistake.[2]

But Beatrice *was* gone—just like Elizabeth. They were here one day and gone the next. Vanished! "Gone to heaven," they said, "slipped away into eternity." But that didn't satisfy me. I was desperate for comfort, equally desperate for an escape from the guilt that pointed to me as the responsible party in a chain of extraordinary circumstances. I wanted answers. The full extent to which I grasped this undertaking I cannot say, but there would be no peace for me until I came to terms with eternity—that forever-and-ever place that had swallowed up and now held both my mothers.

It was a fearful thing to be attracted to this realm of mystery and sadness at nine years of age, and only after two-thirds of my life had been played out would I fully recognize the role these losses would play in my coming to terms with eternity and the God who governed it.

My father, Cecil, was deep in grief and gave me over to the care of his mother, Alma, who had agreed to look after me until he could make other arrangements for my care. She was eager to share her Presbyterian faith, with the intent of comforting me, but as she and Cecil shared little common religious ground, I was caught between two points of view with little comfort. He leaned more to the middle of the road when it came to religion. As far as he was concerned, at least at the moment, heaven and hell were right here. Alma didn't lean at all. It was word for word from the Holy Bible, and that was that! Cecil admitted he didn't have all the answers. He was still searching. That's what people had to do; they had to do their own soul-searching and find the truth for themselves. And so would I.

If he didn't have the answers, how could I ever hope to find them? And what was I to do in the meantime? What if I never found the right answers? I certainly didn't want to go through life with the wrong answers—not when it came to a matter as serious as religion. Either Alma knew what she was talking about or Cecil did. How was I to know which of them was on the right track? It could make a big difference—a terrible difference—if I ended up with the wrong answers.

I decided that religion, like so many things I'd run into, was something I'd have to learn to make the best of. I was resigned to wait for my own answers, but I never stopped wondering or asking, at times to the point of irritating those around me. Now that Beatrice was gone I transferred all my affection onto Cecil and began professing what he professed, continuing to expound many of his searching views into my 30s and 40s, one of these being that God helps those who help themselves. Since God helped only those who helped themselves, the ball was always in my court. How I played it determined God's response, so when things went sour it was always my fault.

If only I had known that God never intended that we live by our own strength, that He purposely created us to live *in need* of Him. While it goes against our human reasoning to remain dependent for the duration of our lives, the only fulfilled people I know are those who have learned to live in a God-dependent partnership. One of the most critical skills we can pass on to our children in our efforts to give them their independence from us is to show them how to depend upon God.

Those I looked to as a child said, "Pull yourself up by your bootstraps and make the best of it." This meant that whatever lay ahead was as threatening as what I'd been through. To be facing a future based on my ability to make the best of it created great anxiety and portrayed an unapproachable and unsympathetic God.

My biggest handicap was always spiritual confusion, too many caretakers with too many differing opinions, the end result being that I became a disciple of *their* opinions. And like those who brought their questions to Jesus, I had no way to sift the error from these opinions because I "knew not the Scriptures, nor the power of God" (Matt. 22:29). I was ignorant of His nature, His will, and His truth, most particularly of His mercy and grace, described by Renal as the two grand pillars of divine administration. If only I'd known that the Bible was written for me, too, and that the Holy Spirit would teach me. Of all the conditions that can befall us, the most tragic is to remain Biblically illiterate.

Has God Really Said?

The intensity with which we pursue spiritual matters depends on what motivates us to begin the search in the first place. Loss and disappointment are powerful motivators and will steer us down one of two paths. One leads to truth, the other sends us wandering through a maze of theories, always speculating but never finding the confidence that comes from experiencing the truth for ourselves.

It isn't so much the number of choices which prevents us from deciding between these two paths, but that we do not respond well to either/or situations when it comes to the spiritual realm. We are easily seduced by the philosophy of many paths leading to the same destination because it gives us an option to work it out *our* way.

Then, if we become disenchanted with one way, we can always try another way and will find plenty of people willing to introduce us to *their* way. And, if we happen to be one of those who puts God on trial—convicting Him on the evidence of our circumstances— we can always find a reason for listening to other voices. But the question is always the same: "Has God really said . . . ?" Here we take our place beside Eve, not to consider what God said concerning the forbidden fruit but the comfort and ease of the path: "Has God really said there is but one way and One mediator between God and man?"

When we consider that the laws of physics and aerodynamics operate only one way, the stars and planets have but one way mapped out for them, and the seasons adhere to their one-way cycles, we observe a one-way universe created by a one-way God. His way! But rather than be thankful for the stability this provides us, we buck the one-way system and search for *another* way of ordering our individual lives—one less restricting—or the one our friends have decided upon.

> Without a doubt, the mightiest thought the mind can entertain is the thought of God. . . . That He *is*, what He is *like;* and what we as moral beings must do about Him. . . . Were we able to extract from any man a complete answer to the question, "What comes to mind when you think about God?" we might predict with certainty the spiritual future of that individual.[3]
>
> —A. W. Tozer

It bears repeating that what we believe becomes the truth we are going to live by, even if what we profess as truth is founded on deception, and it seems that a number of us would rather build a case for our own confusion than yield to an either/or decision. We don't want anything or *anyone* impinging on our freedom *even if it be God Himself!* It's much easier to live with options than with once-and-for-all decisions, particularly when there are strings attached to those decisions.

I am indebted to a merciful God, Who ordained my times, and to His people of faith who were as tools to whittle me into His purpose. I think of Alma McGregor, a staunch Presbyterian, laying the first caring brick in the foundation of my faith when she taught me that God was sovereign; it would be His will and not mine that would rule my life. I remember with affection the nuns—who, as a non-Catholic I once resented—who seeded in me the hope of things to come when they showed me a movie about the life of Christ.

It takes time to get the rest of the story, to come to terms with why God allows what He allows in some lives but disallows in others, to give up the need to understand why it worked out the way it did. Belief and trust in God are often two very distant frames of mind for those who struggle with issues of the past. There was no question that I believed in God, but acknowledging His existence and trusting in Him were miles apart in my thinking.

Dr. T. DeWitt Talmage tells of a small boy who was flying a kite that soared so high it was almost out of sight. A gentleman happened by and saw the boy holding the string and looking very intently upward. "What have you there?" he asked. "A kite, sir," the boy answered. "A kite," said the gentleman, "how can that be? I don't see it." The boy responded with, "Ah, but I can feel it tugging, sir."

I felt the tug of God as a child, but not until my late 40s was I at ease with the One behind the tug. I can only speculate as to the impact the following allegory might have had on me had it been available when I was young and unable to understand the Bible. You may find yourself someplace in this story. Whatever effect it may have on you, it is my prayer that it will lead you to a serious study of the Scriptures that inspired it.

THE KING'S TEARS

Once upon a time, in the City of Disappointments, there lived many known by the name of Broken-and-Wounded. And high above the City was the Kingdom of Peace, ruled by the King of all that ever was or ever shall be. No one became a citizen of the Kingdom of Peace except by choice, and no one willing to pledge allegiance to the King was ever turned away.

Next to the King's great white throne was a vessel of translucent pearl. An angel, known as the Keeper of Tears, stood beside the vessel. His was a very sacred duty indeed, for the vessel contained the tears shed by those known by the name of Broken-and-Wounded. Since the beginning of all that ever was or ever shall be, there was never a day when the angels failed to gather tears for the King, and never a day when He was not present as the tears were measured and recorded.

And the King grieved for the people. It was never His plan that they should suffer so. Suffering entered the City after the angels of darkness, led by the Deceiver, were banished from the Kingdom. From that time on their only ambition was to interfere with the destiny of the people in the City. And so it was that the enemies of the King became the enemies of the people.

Then it came to pass that the King came to the City to teach the people how to live according to the Kingdom of Peace. Some would not listen, but those who did preserved His truth for all who would come after them. With every generation there were those who loved the King and accepted His plan for the good of all. Those who scoffed at the King's ways fell under the rule of the avenging angels of darkness and walked in *their* ways.

The avenging angels, being wise to human behavior, continued to prey upon the people until the Kingdom of Darkness began to manifest within families. Husbands were harsh with their wives. Women were provoked to anger. Children became discouraged, fearful, and rebellious. Indifference and pride gave way to anger and violence; families were torn apart as the wounds of one generation were handed down to the next generation.

Those who remained loyal to the King told and retold all He had accomplished during His time in the City. One of these stories concerned a young woman whose heart was hardened against the King because of the many abuses she had suffered. One day the King spoke to her, saying:

"Listen my child! My words will be as life to you if you will heed them. I hear your cries for justice, but you must leave justice to Me. Why do you judge Me for what *man* has done to you? Have you not heard how the avenging angels work their evil through those who harden their hearts against Me?

"You long for peace, but you will never find it apart from Me. My love is far more powerful than any sorrow that has befallen you; My hand many times stronger than the evil that manipulates you. I offer refreshment for your soul and a reward for your sorrow that is far greater than what you have suffered.

"Do not think that because I ask you to forgive those who have harmed you that I regard your wounds lightly. I have recorded and saved all of your tears. I have grieved for your afflictions and suffered them with you. It is for *your* sake that you must forgive. Bitterness holds you hostage to the past and continually stirs up your pain."

As the young woman stood in the presence of the King, her hope was restored. No longer would she measure the King's love by her circumstances or blame Him for the cruelty of others. Never again would she question His ways, but trust Him to transform what was meant for evil into something beautiful for His purpose and her eternal benefit; for this was the promise to those who put their trust in Him. She treasured the King's words in her heart and went about the City to encourage others known by the name of Broken-and-Wounded. It was in the telling of such stories that the people learned of the love of a King who saved tears in a beautiful vessel.

The battle for the destiny of the people continued until it appeared that an entire generation would be swept into the Kingdom of Darkness, for just as some served as agents of hope for the cause of the King, there were those who served as agents for the Deceiver. So it came to pass that there came upon the City a time of great fascination with angels, with no discernment between the two Kingdoms in which they operated. More and more people were intent on doing what was right in their own eyes, with no regard for the danger of living by the law of the Kingdom of Darkness.

From age to age the Keeper of Tears carried out his duties, knowing that as surely as he had witnessed the beginning of evil, he would witness the end of evil. How often he longed to inquire of the King as to the hour of reckoning, but he kept his silence, for only the King knew the day and the hour when all who would choose to live in the Kingdom of Peace had made their decision. Only then would He take up His sword.

Then there came a time of such evil that the Keeper of Tears sensed the new beginning and began to measure the days by the condition of the City. Fathers deserted the home. The unborn and the elderly were no longer valued. Perversion of every kind was published and practiced openly. There was no honor to be found in those elected to govern the City. Violent children roamed the streets, the prisons were filled, and there was little room left in the vessel for the King's tears.

Surely the appointed time was at hand! At any moment the heavens would echo with the thundering of horses as the angels of justice, led by the King, descended upon the City. Soon the angelic hosts were speaking in hushed voices about the coming battle. Excitement spread to every corner of the Kingdom. Even the King's horse, set aside from the very beginning, grew restless and ran at increasing speeds. He reared high into the air, eyes fierce with anticipation, sensing that his hour was close at hand. Never had there been such a horse as this—a brave and noble horse—fit only for a King. And none but the King of all that ever was or ever shall be would sit upon the back of this dazzling white steed, the very one foretold in the final pages of the Record of the King.

To this very day the angelic hosts are poised and ready for the signal that will bring an end to the Kingdom of Darkness. On that day the Deceiver, along with his avenging angels and those who served with them, will be taken captive and banished to the Land of No Return. Then the King will proclaim the end of evil and the end of sorrow and tears. Once again He will live among the people in the City, and there will come a time of peace such as has never been known before. All these things have been foretold in the Record of the King. They shall come to pass!

And after the old things are passed away, the Keeper of Tears will seal up the vessel and place it in the center of the Kingdom of Peace—where it will remain for all eternity—as a reminder of the love of the King for those once known as Broken-And-Wounded.

We are born into conflict, but not without resources. God has made provision for us by way of an arsenal of truth which is readily available to those who will honestly seek it. How encouraging it is to know that God grieves with us, that our circumstances are no indication of His love, and that in Him we find all we need to face any situation.

If you are living with regrets and the grief of *what might have been*, it is never too late to give God the broken pieces of your past and ask Him to make something beautiful out of them for His glory and your eternal happiness.

Notes

1. A. W. Tozer, *Knowledge of the Holy* (New York: HarperCollins Publishers, 1961), 1.
2. Donna Ferguson, *The Someday Kid* (Summerland, Calif.: Harbor House [West], 1993), 17.
3. A. W. Tozer, *Knowledge of the Holy* (New York: HarperCollins Publishers, 1961), 2.

2

FAITH AND CIRCUMSTANCES

When it comes to taking advice from those who have never been in our situation, we tend to discount most of what they say. "If you haven't been where I've been, you can't possibly understand what I'm going through." Robert Burns confirmed this train of thought when he wrote: "Misery is like love; to speak its language truly, the author must have felt it."

One gains a perspective into emotional healing after overcoming a history of an alcoholic father, the suicide of a mother, foster homes, abuse, the loss of adoptive parents, institutional life, the birth of a mentally retarded child, and the desertion of a spouse.

When you have experienced the power of the past to dictate the future, you want to wave a red flag and shout: Look out! Deal with it. Don't shut God out of it. Your life is too precious to waste!

The topic of suffering threatens believers and unbelievers alike. Some will say that if we get the sin out of our lives we can avoid suffering; others support the notion that saying the right words the right way obligates God to remove our suffering. An example of one of the most blatant violations of the holy intentions of God in respect to suffering is seen in the following incident: Dave Reover, a severely scarred Vietnam veteran turned evangelist, was preaching in a church when several in the congregation walked out. One of them stopped to say, before the entire assembly, that if Dave would "get the sin out of his life God would take away his scars."[1]

What do we say to those who serve God as a result of their wounds? What do we say to this war-scarred veteran, or to Joni Erickson Tada, a woman who attends to the work of God throughout the world from a wheelchair? How do we show our appreciation for these soldiers of the Cross whose bodies bear the evidence of yesterday's tragedy? We thank them for persevering and encouraging us by their example!

THE HIGHWAY TO HEAVEN

Some attempt to defend God's position when it comes to the issue of suffering, using one Scripture to invalidate another. If God, in the Person of Jesus Christ, suffered for our sake, we should not be surprised when we suffer. If the Holy Spirit is grieved, how can we expect to escape our portion? Our Lord told us we would have tribulation (John 16:33).

But, some argue, weren't we promised protection? Yes, and the presence of distress in our lives does not negate that protection. God has a plan that reaches far beyond these few short years into a destiny of such proportion that we can barely wrap our thoughts around it. Getting a handle on eternity does not call for a giant stretch of the imagination, but rather the earnest search for those things having to do with it. What God plans for one life will not be the same as for another. We are encouraged to "run with patient endurance *and* steady *and* active persistence the appointed course of the race that is set before us" (Heb. 12:1).

The Holy Spirit is leading all Christians toward the same finish line, but the course planned for one runner differs from that of another. This is essential to our understanding of suffering in the context of our eternal destiny.

Can we close our eyes to the accounts of those who suffered in Jesus' day and say they are not relevant to those of us in this present age? In John 9:2 Jesus answers the Jews concerning a man blind from birth, explaining the reasons for his blindness, "that the works of God might be made manifest in him."

We know that without faith it is impossible to please God (Heb. 11:6), but to infer that when our situations do not change it is always due to a lack of faith on our part places a heavy burden on many.

The Apostle Paul was not lacking in faith. He had faith enough to risk his life for the Gospel, to endure years of imprisonment and martyrdom. Joseph remained faithful to God when he was sold into slavery and imprisoned for something he did not do. In saying, "You thought evil against me, but God meant it for good," Joseph does more than suggest God's hand held back for a time (Gen. 50:20). Like Paul, he suffered for the benefit of a nation, and as an example and encouragement to us. Our afflictions are not likely to play out in such proportions as those of Paul and Joseph, but we can be assured that God's intentions toward us are always for our eternal good and His eternal purposes.

WHERE WERE YOU, LORD?

When Lazarus died, Martha cried, "Master, if you had been here, my brother would not have died" (John 11:21). In raising Lazarus from the dead, our Lord demonstrated the power of God in a way never seen before, and what happened then continues to speak to us today. My cry was, "Lord, if you had been there my mother would still be alive, my father would never have abandoned me, my son would not be retarded, my husband would never have deserted us."

What is there in your history that causes you to say, "Lord, if you had been there . . . ?" As Jesus called Lazarus from the tomb so long ago, He is calling us out of the tombs of our past, so that the works of God may also be manifest in our lives.

A woman was blaming God for not changing the circumstances in her family. I told her it was not God's fault that her father was an alcoholic. "But He allowed it, didn't He? What's the difference?" This is a threatening question. How can we trust a God who *allowed* our damaging years? Is there a difference between causing or allowing something to happen? Yes, there is. And it is a significant difference. If anyone was keeping track, we would no doubt prove the oldest question in the history of man to be, "How could God allow this to happen?"

Yet there is a far more profound question to consider. Why would God, when He could have abolished suffering altogether, choose instead to enter into suffering with us? All we can say to this is—we don't know! He does not explain everything to us anymore than we explain everything about life to a preschooler. There are some places off-limits to our understanding. We must learn to respect God's boundaries in faith. "The secret things belong unto the Lord our God, but the things which are revealed belong to us." (Deut. 29:29).

We are not completely without reasons for the problem of evil. Some deliberately choose evil. Some believe in God but are not willing to make room for Him in their lives. There are dark spiritual forces working against us. Then, as Proverbs 19:3 tells us, we may ruin our lives by our own foolishness and then *blame it on the Lord!* In John 5:14 Jesus speaks to the man He has just healed. "See, you are well! Stop sinning or something worse may happen to you." When we operate outside the perimeter of God's will, whether we act out of ignorance or premeditated rebellion, the end result is tribulation, for someone.

We reap what we sow . . . as sure as the law of gravity keeps the planets on track . . . so our actions and our lives are connected by a thousand invisible threads, along these sympathetic fibers our actions run as causes and return to us as results.

—Herman Melville

When it comes to childhood issues we are always looking for a place to pin the blame. As children we most often pointed the finger at ourselves. Grownups had all the power, so they were always right. If fault was to be found it was in us. The answer, if we could find it, would give us a reason to say it wasn't our fault. We could then point to somebody else, transfer the guilt onto them, and be relieved of the shame of the past.

Our Lord has felt our grief as surely as that of Mary and Martha that day so long ago. God had His reasons for allowing Lazarus to die. He has His reasons for not intervening at certain times the way we would have liked, but I have never met the person yet who, when asked to come up with a time God did intervene on their behalf, has not been able to do so.

The apostle Paul wrote of a time when his prayers were not answered in the way he would have liked.

To keep me from becoming conceited because of these surpassingly great revelations, there was given me a thorn in my flesh, a messenger of Satan to torment me. Three times I pleaded with the Lord to take it away from me. But he said to me, "My grace is sufficient for you, for my power is made perfect in weakness" (2 Cor. 12:7–9 NIV).

How easily Paul could have turned proud and boastful, forgetting (as we are prone to do) that without Christ he could do nothing. In the 11th chapter of Hebrews, referred to as faith's hall of fame, we read of those who "through faith" lived to see the promises of God fulfilled in their lives; however, in verses 36 through 40 we also read of the nameless *others* who held fast to the promises in spite of great suffering, even unto death, yet never received them.

Dr. J. Sidlow Baxter writes, "The very things which seem to break us are the things which really make us. It is supremely important that we relate this problem of pain to our *ultimate destiny*. . . . Pain, suffering, adversity, do something of eternal significance to our character, according to the way we react to them."[2]

We can praise God for His promises although we may not yet have experienced the fulfillment of His promises. I've seen some of those promises manifested in my life, but as a result of suffering, I've also learned that God gives greater cause for celebration than the cost of our suffering. This is what we are called to share with those who have yet to discover this truth. Yes, God answers prayer. He does heal. He still works miracles. He is merciful and abounding with love. But let us never forget that He is sovereign! There is pain involved in this holy occupation we call the Christian life. And there is pain in emotional healing. We do our Lord a disservice to suggest otherwise.

God will transform hardships into eternal dividends when we place them in His capable hands. We cannot change what has already happened, but we can cooperate with Him to convert those experiences into the fruit of our lives. With this understanding, we can embrace Romans 8:28 in anticipation of the completed work of verse 29:

> We are assured *and* know that [God being a partner in
> their labor] all things work together *and* are [fitting into
> a plan] for good to *and* for those who love God and are

called according to [His] design *and* purpose. For those whom He foreknew [of whom He was aware and loved beforehand], He also destined from the beginning [foreordaining them] to be molded into the image of His Son [and share inwardly His likeness], that He might become the firstborn among many brethren.

The good toward which all things are working is the remaking of our character to resemble the character of Christ. Here we find cause for celebration, knowing that as a result of these trying times we are carved out, polished, and given a new and an *eternal* likeness.

Consider this: an eternal purpose has been reserved for you in God's grand scheme of things. He longs to conform you to fit the specific purpose that bears your name. If you can lay hold of this truth, whatever you've been through—whatever you are presently facing—is diminished by comparison to the everlasting purpose secured for you before the world was spoken into existence. It is here that the discomfort of God's conforming work makes way for His conforming purpose.

We are born into a hostile environment to face the challenges that will shape our history. Our mind becomes the slate upon which everyone we come in contact with will write their opinions. We are bombarded by voices through music, media, school, and social interactions, and it is from this ongoing stream of information that we form our opinions and make our decisions: what to keep and what to toss out; what crowd we want to be identified with; what political party; what occupation, lifestyle, and code of ethics; even what we wear, drive, and how we play. We want to fit in, to be loved, and to belong.

We don't choose the circumstances into which we are born,

and because we are molded by our history, we often make poor choices that then become the heritage of our sons and daughters. None of us can live our lives to the exclusion of others. The family unit remains intact even if we are emotionally or geographically separated. It is an attachment and an influence that reaches beyond the grave.

Coming to terms with what ails us is never easy. Some of us pretend it really doesn't bother us all that much and try to dissolve our pain in positive thinking. I counted my blessings. After all, my name wasn't Helen Keller. I had the benefit of all five senses. I escaped the polio epidemic when many of my generation were not so fortunate. As long as there was something to be thankful for, there was nothing to deal with. Those psychological trenches might still be in place had God not coaxed out of hiding the little girl I used to be and forced me to come to terms with her *and* with Him. In so doing she never had to go back into hiding, and I could stop wrestling with the memories of the way it used to be.

Pleasant and unpleasant memories remain tucked away in the brain; both can be retrieved under the right conditions. As we approach traditional holidays we remember how it was when we were children. Just the smell of something baking in the oven, a scent in the air in the spring, a piece of music on the radio—these are the things that memories are made of. The same holidays and sensory sensations will also trigger painful memories. It is how we react to these memories that tells us where we are in the healing process.

If your family members or other caretakers were emotionally impoverished, you will be affected. Yet in spite of actual abuse, neglect, and any number of other social diseases that infect the home, it *is* possible to grow up under these circumstances and appear to manage quite well. Like the chameleon who changes color to blend in with the environment, we adapted to the surroundings, people, and situations so as to incur the least damage to ourselves. The problem arises when we fail to recognize that our former methods of survival are no longer appropriate and can actually sabotage our happiness now and interfere with our relationship with God.

Sometimes we rise above our circumstances; sometimes we don't. When we attempt to bypass the legitimate pain of revising the outcome of our lives, we shut God out of the very area where we need Him the most, to the extent that we may become instruments of grief for others. There are no perfect families, no perfect childhoods, and no perfect storybook lives. This is why we must continually look to the perfection in Christ and avail ourselves of the remedy He purchased on our behalf at Calvary.

As Milton wrote, "As the morning tells the day, so the childhood tells the man." It also tells the woman, her relationships with men and the next generation, because the hand that rocks the cradle has always wielded a great deal of influence. In our attempts to survive we can end up being the person we are the most deceived about, and it is through this distortion that we attempt to establish families of our own. When we deal honestly with our emotional baggage, everyone around us will also benefit.

A Good Investment

The question is not CAN we recover, but are we willing to do what it TAKES to recover? Are we willing to *invest* in the future to the extent that what happened to us will not control what we do now? Psychological band-aids lose their adhesive very quickly. All my striving and the best intentions of a therapist were not enough to relieve me of my emotional pain. I benefited from the insights therapy offered, but understanding why I was the way I was did not recover me.

The difference between those able to shake the distortion of the past and those who never make it out of their history is a spiritual difference, made possible by a spiritual transaction. People will spend a lifetime in recovery if they are blind to the Person behind the transaction. Only God can make this happen, because He IS the transaction. Only in Him can we find relief for those areas stunted or warped through negative life experiences.

If our history has been damaging, we have a choice. Will God become our excuse or our hope? Will we spend our lives nursing our wounds or invite Him to develop His life within us? You and I must take our histories to the Cross for confession and healing *before we can visit the empty tomb*. Emotional wounds can separate us from the life-giving love of God if we do nothing about them. It is in complete surrender and dependence upon Christ that we find authentic happiness. This is what He taught, this is what He lived, and this is what each of us has longed for since our first howling breath!

> Who is it that is victorious over [who conquers] the world but he who believes that Jesus is the Son of God [who adheres to, trusts in, and relies on that fact] (1 John 5:5)?

We know that Satan is the instigator of evil as the one who first violated God's law in heaven. Since that time he seeks to destroy what God loves most: US! We also know that God cannot and will not reverse His physical laws of creation. If you jump off a ten-story building, you're dead the minute you hit the pavement because you violated the law of gravity. If somebody pushes you the results will be the same, except in this case you had nothing to do with it. Wounded people are the casualties of a spiritual war that rages around us 24 hours a day and the outcome of turning our backs on God.

But there comes a time when we can no longer plead our unfortunate circumstances, our fragile human nature, or the enemies of our souls; we cannot blame our parents, our mates, or our children. We must humble ourselves and admit that we, too, have failed and are in need of a Savior.

Under New Management

When we experience God—and we can—we are no longer managed by the past because faith now becomes the manager. And as our faith is in God in the Person of Jesus Christ, we are managed by Him rather than the evil that fostered our losses and failures. However, it is misleading to say that there is a quick fix to emotional healing. We cannot run people through a hurt detector and expect them to walk away free of the effects of the wounds of their childhood. The same applies to the loss of a spouse or a child. There is no way to escape the legitimate pain of recovery. We must grieve our losses. And grieving hurts! It is also a friend. It was grief that taught me to be honest with myself and with God.

The grief of the past can be compared to the pain an amputee feels in the limb that is no longer there. The amputee cannot grow another limb. We cannot reconstruct our past. But both the amputee and the emotionally bruised can recover from their limitations with God's help. But unless we know the name and character of the God we are depending on, we have no place to go with our grief.

God with Us

The sufferings of our Lord are not limited to the time spent on the Cross. Do you think He has forgotten the Cross? Is He not aware of those who are suffering today because of their sins and the sins of others perpetrated upon them? He continues to bear our suffering with us. In the words of an unknown fifteenth-century writer:

> God did not come into the world to explain suffering like some philosopher. Nor did He come to erase it as He could have done. But rather He came to take that suffering and fill it with His presence.

God could have brought me to where I am today by any number of ways. Why He allowed what He allowed is His business. I have stopped questioning His methods because I have reaped the benefits of His methods. I understand what Job meant when he said, "My ears had heard of You but now my eyes have seen You" (Job 42:5).

When I look back over my journey, I see loss for loss turned into spiritual treasure, every disappointment exchanged for spiritual privilege. I will keep these memories polished with gratitude and praise. God forbid that I should grow cold and forgetful! As the Israelites were commanded to keep the Passover in memory of their great deliverance, I want to celebrate and keep alive all that God has done for me.

Once we have experienced the grace of God, we have an explanation for the hope that is in us (1 Peter 3:15). Knowing He has brought us this far, we are confident He will take us the rest of the way. This is what guards the ground we have already gained and supplies us for the remainder of the journey. Our strength comes from maintaining the strength already received—by holding on to what we have laid hold of in the past—by means of an attitude of gratitude that is stronger than anything we are currently facing. It comes from the knowledge that God never changes, so that when life doesn't live up to our expectations, or when God doesn't answer in the way we would like Him to, we will not be moved.

I have strength for all things in Christ Who empowers me [I am ready for anything and equal to anything through Him Who infuses inner strength into me; I am self-sufficient in Christ's sufficiency] (Phil. 4:13).

In his classic poem, *The Hound of Heaven,* Francis Thompson presents a valid perspective not often expounded upon today.

> All which I took from thee I did but take,
> Not for thy harms,
> But just that thou might'st seek it in My arms.
> Rise, clasp My hand, and come.

Christian history is rich with the lives of those who overcame by the leading of the same nail-scarred hands that beckon each of us.

Don't allow your past to become the mother of your children, the mistress of your household, or the other woman in your marriage.

Notes

1. As seen on the Trinity Broadcast Network's *Praise the Lord* program.
2. J. Sidlow Baxter, *Awake My Heart* (Grand Rapids, Mich.: Zondervan Publishing House, 1960), 318.

3

LIVING WITH REGRETS

✠

Most of us live with regrets of one kind or another. The one that heads my list is that I waited so long to undertake a serious study of the Bible on my own, rather than reading it in bits and pieces and relying solely on Sunday sermons. There are many in the church today who think, as I once did, that I'd found all there was to find. I had no idea that conversion was but the first step in the process of being a Christian.

I'd followed Jesus to the best of my ability since age 11. I was baptized at 17 and went forward in a Billy Graham crusade at 26. As one of the first to reach the platform when the invitation was given, I stood directly in front of the podium and repeated the sinner's prayer. I have never forgotten the urgency in this preacher's voice or in his eyes, and I count this as the most significant day of my life. The faith of my childhood had reached an official status. I'd come to God, accepted His terms for my eternal future, and publicly committed myself to Christ. I was on my way to heaven!

But like those who set out for America aboard the *Titanic,* I was on a collision course with something greater than I was prepared to handle because I remained ignorant of the *purpose* of the journey—that is, to make the crossing as a disciple of Christ, not as one who hears only, but as one who participates in the things heard.

The *Titanic* was presumed to be unsinkable. Laying aside the theories as to the structural integrity of the ship, we can still point to the breakdown in communications as the main cause of the tragedy. In spite of eight separate warnings from other ships in the area concerning the ice field up ahead, the *Titanic* never altered her course. When the final message was received, the wireless operator, exhausted after 14 hours of transmitting messages for first-class passengers, interrupted the transmission, saying, "Shut up, shut up, I'm busy." Nobody "got" that message either.

If somebody had been listening, the iceberg could have been avoided! If somebody had prepared for the unexpected, there would have been sufficient seating in the lifeboats to preserve an additional 1,502 souls.

The passengers put their trust in the Captain and assumed they were safe. When it comes to the intentions of God, we cannot assume that all Captains who stand behind the pulpit are steering their congregations into safe waters. In his book *How To Be Born Again*, Billy Graham expresses the need for the church to recover the authoritative Biblical message. "Thousands of untaught Christians are being deceived today, as are millions of people who are rejecting and ignoring the true Christ. Deceivers with intellectual arguments which are wound like the epitome of scholarship are beguiling many."[1]

Jesus said, "I have come as a light into the world, so that whoever believes on Me—Who cleaves to *and* trusts in *and* relies on Me—may not continue to live in darkness." (John 12:46). I thought I'd been doing just that. Wasn't that what the church was for? Wasn't I already living the Christian life? Then how did Satan get his hooks into our family?

I didn't know it at the time, but I was still living in darkness. I believed in Christ, but remained a disciple of my own opinions, based on what I'd acquired from those no more enlightened than myself, and the religious trappings of a diluted Christianity. The same was true of my husband, Martin. We sat beside each other in a church for 20 years, listening to more philosophy and psychology than Scripture, and because *we failed to seek the things of God on our own*, as God's Word makes clear we are to do, we suffered the consequences, as did our children.

We will be navigating around icebergs as long as we live and are more likely than not to collide with a few. Without an understanding of God as revealed in the Old and New Testaments, we endanger ourselves and our loved ones now and in the future. And, if we remain disciples of our own opinions rather than disciples of Christ, we will never be able to discern between the truth of God or the lies of Satan.

Doubt is always easier to come by than faith, especially if your trust in people is destroyed early in life. Add to this the influence of other opinions as to the authenticity of the Bible, and doubt has another ally with which to strengthen its position; when these opinions are generated by significant family members, they become rooted in our thinking.

In spite of a sincere Christian conversion experience, I continued to struggle with the damaging years, hoping that someday I could "outlive" them. While I felt bonded to Christ through my suffering, I saw Him as a victim like myself, and remained estranged from the Father who allowed Him to go to the Cross, and, I was sure, had condemned me to my own. Up to this time I was acquainted with a partial Gospel. It wasn't just that something was missing, but that *Somebody* was missing. William Barclay warns us of the danger in taking the experience of conversion to mean the end of the road, and of interpreting the experience to mean we are now completed and perfected Christians.

> Conversion cannot stop at confronting a man with the
> Cross, even if it must begin there. It must go on to tell

a man of the Risen Christ, of the power of the Spirit, of the new life which the Spirit makes possible . . . unless he lays hold upon the power of the Holy Spirit, unless the Holy Spirit daily lives more in him and he in the Holy Spirit, then the experience of conversion will necessarily lead to nowhere but disappointment, disillusionment and frustration.[2]

We need not get lost in the mysteries of the Trinity to experience the power of the Holy Spirit; and it will be to the good of our souls to go to the Bible and to meditate on what the Bible says about the work of the Spirit of God in the lives of men, in order that we may lay hold of that power for our own lives.[3]

I don't remember a specific moment when the Holy Spirit began to teach me, only that I was consumed with a spiritual hunger. All I wanted to hear about, talk about, and read about was Jesus. I now understood that God always intended I study the Bible for myself, and that He would instruct me. And I was finally in a position to learn.

Nobody was more surprised than I was to find Jesus in the Old Testament. The One who spoke from the burning bush and parted the Red Sea was the same One I'd been hanging on to all these years. He was not only the Son of God—He was God the Son! Heaven's arithmetic which presents one God in three Persons is beyond me. But the truth of the revelation of Jesus Christ is no longer a mystery. It is the truth by which I live. It is by this same truth that I was able to recover from the damaging years and experience real joy for the first time in my life. The same truth and joy are waiting for those who will actively seek it. Anyone who honestly looks for God IN the Bible will find Him.

J. I. Packer writes, "Once you become aware that the main business that you are here for is to know God, most of life's problems fall into place of their own accord. What makes life worthwhile is having a big-enough objective, something which catches our imagination and lays hold of our allegiance; and this the Christian has, in a way that no other man has. For what higher, more exalted and more compelling goal can there be than to know God?"[4]

Many of us fail to recognize how our experiences can cloud our perception of God. We may even go so far as to put ourselves on the receiving end of a punishing stick carved out of our misconceptions concerning Him. The defeated soul needs a reason to try again. Christ gives us the reason. He IS the reason!

The following is a paraphrase of the Scriptures which revealed how God felt about me all those years I thought He was against me. This is the *knowing* that began my recovery. As you read, remember these are also His thoughts toward YOU.

My eye is on my daughter. I see her tears. I have recorded them and saved them in my bottle. Though she thought My hand was against her, I will reward her sorrow doublefold. Though she has sown in tears she will reap in gladness and rejoice in her lot. I will be her buckler and her shield. Though the floods and the flames threaten her, they will not destroy her. I am near to the downtrodden and the crushed in spirit. Like a mother I will comfort her. I will part the waters for her and restore the years the locust has stolen. I will reveal my Son to her and He will be in the yoke with her.

Then I will do a new thing: I will make a path in her wilderness and rivers in her desert, and she will know that from the day that I began to knit her together in her mother's womb, I have had a plan, a plan to give her a future and a hope. I have created her and I will carry her. I will instruct her in the way she should go, and I will watch over her. I have made her a joint heir with My Son. I have prepared a place for her so that where We dwell, there she may dwell also.

The love in those passages can still move me to tears, the love that never gave up on me, the love that sought me when I couldn't find it on my own. Wherever you are today, whatever your circumstances, be assured this same love is also seeking you.

We are often blinded to the love of God when we are grieving the loss of love. We may even resist His consolation because the longing to be accepted by those who don't return our feelings is more important to us at the moment. A woman who has just learned of her husband's involvement with another woman has a difficult time taking comfort from God. What she wants most at this time is the love of her husband. Nothing my adoptive mother said could make me happy to be in her home. I wasn't there because she wanted me, but because I wasn't wanted someplace else. There was no comfort in being with her when I so desperately wanted to be with my father.

In coming to terms with negative experiences, the love of God is often beyond our grasp in the beginning, as are His remedies. All we can feel at this stage is the loss. We need to remember that the heart of God is wrenched with ours when life overwhelms us.

By Invitation Only

I've learned not to let what I don't understand about God undermine what I *do* understand. To those who seek Him is given increased understanding, but we will always be learning, because He is the most inexhaustible study we can undertake, the most exciting, and the most rewarding. The invitation of Christ recorded in Matthew 11:28–29 tells us *how* we are to learn:

Come unto Me all you who labor and are heavy laden
and overburdened, and I will cause you to rest. Take My
Yoke upon you, and learn of Me. . .

When we receive an invitation, if we have any manners at all,
we will respond. Yet how easily we lay aside the personal invita-
tions extended by the Lord of the Universe. One day as I medi-
tated on this passage, I was suddenly compelled to respond in a
personal and direct way. I told the Lord I wanted His yoke. I
wanted to learn of Him, from Him, and gain the refreshment
promised to those who respond to His invitation. I knelt down
and with tears of gratitude received His yoke.

Let this invitation be a continual reminder that it is our Lord
Who bears the heaviest portion of the life committed to Him. The
way *is* narrow, often dangerous, but once yoked with Christ we
can be assured that He will custom-fit His yoke to make it compatible with our particular journey. As the young and inexperi-
enced ox was yoked together with the more experienced ox in
Biblical times, we begin our training in the ways of God once we
are yoked with our Savior.

Christ did not come with a single objective. He came not only
to save us, but to reveal the character of God *and* to conscript us
into His Kingdom. In taking the yoke of Christ we actually take
up the cause of Christ. He has already taken up our cause. We *are*
His cause! And in attempting to move beyond the effects of our
damaging years we need, above all else, what the yoke provides. It
is the yoke that causes all things to work together to adapt us to
all we were created to be. As Elton Trueblood put it:

> The central call to Christian commitment is phrased in
> the words "take My yoke upon you." The terms are the
> terms of recruitment.[5]

When we choose to make ourselves available to God, all the benefits of our Lord's life and death are made available to us. This is the relationship He desires for us and the one we ought to desire. I've learned that when my "want to" and my "ought to" resist acting in accordance to the will of God and in my best interest, asking Him to help me do what He requires of me is the best way to go about getting there.

I considered many opinions during my search for wholeness. Each time I thought I'd found what was going to "fix" me, I came across another book with another opinion, and in trying to form my own opinions from the opinions of the so-called experts, I came to the same conclusion as Phillips Brooks:

> Call your opinion your creed, and you will change it
> every week. Make your creed simply and broadly out of
> the revelation of God, and you may keep it to the end.

If we insist on a comfortable faith, we will gravitate to those who support our view of God in the way we imagine Him to be. We will always be exchanging ideas with those who see it our way. Quoting from Billy Graham once more: "Throughout time . . . whether ancient or modern, all have posed alternatives to the Biblical way of approaching God. Men and women may devise plans to satisfy their inner longings, but in the midst of all the religions of the world God's way is available in the Bible for all who will come to Him on His terms."[6]

I once shared my faith with a woman I'd not seen in 30 years. Her response was, "Oh, I tried that for a while, but it didn't work." She saw faith as a positive thinking wheel that after so many spins was supposed to change things, but after seeing no change for the better, she went on to pursue other paths, none of which has brought her any closer to God or made her any happier than she was 30 years ago.

The God of Abraham, Isaac, and Jacob asks us what He asked of Peter: "Who do you say that I am?" (Matt. 16:15). Until we recognize God in the Person of Jesus Christ and what His life provides for us today, our search for emotional healing will amount to no more than the plodding of a donkey after a carrot at the end of a stick. We can spend a lifetime *reaching* for restoration, but like the donkey in pursuit of the carrot, we will never taste it.

We do not have to go to seminary to understand the Bible. We have been given the Spirit, the Author Himself. Matthew Henry said that to understand a book the reader must know the same language as the author: "He must in many cases have somewhat of the same spirit in which the author wrote. To understand the Scriptures, we need the same Holy Spirit dwelling in us which enabled holy men of old to write them."[7] God rewards those who diligently seek Him (Heb. 11:6). Those who don't are destined to live and die with regrets.

> So I say to you, Ask *and* keep on asking and it shall be given you; seek *and* keep on seeking and you shall find; knock *and* keep on knocking and the door shall be opened to you. For everyone who asks *and* keeps on asking receives; and he who seeks *and* keeps on seeking finds; and to him who knocks *and* keeps on knocking, the door shall be opened (Luke 11:9-10).

> Almighty God, grant us wisdom and revelation into the mysteries of your Word so that we might grow in our knowledge of You. Flood our hearts with light so that we can understand and appreciate the future You have called us to share with You. And enable us through the power of Your Spirit to encourage those who do not yet know You. (see Eph. 1:17-19)

Notes

1. Billy Graham, *How To Be Born Again* (Nashville, Tenn.: World Books, 1977), 61. All rights reserved.
2. William Barclay, *The Promise of the Spirit* (Epworth Press; used by permission of Methodist Publishing House, 20 Ivatt Way, Peterborough, PE3 7PG, England, 1960), 111.
3. Ibid., 11.
4. J. I. Packer, *Knowing God,* (Downers Grove, Ill: Intervarsity Press, 1973), 29, 30.
5. Elton Trueblood, *The Yoke of Christ and Other Sermons* (New York: HarperCollins Publishers, 1958), 13.
6. Graham, *How To Be Born Again,* 64.
7. Andrew Murray, *The Spirit of Jesus Christ,* (London: James Nisbett & Co., London, 1908), 50.

4

This Thing Called Love

When my daughters asked me how they would know if they were really in love, I told them what I was told as a girl: "I can't explain it, but you'll know when it happens to you."

"But how will I know he's the one I should marry?" I mumbled something like, "You'll recognize the right one when he comes along," knowing at the time that this would prove as useless to them as it was when someone gave it to me. If I had it to do over again, they would get an entirely different answer. And I'd like to think that I could shelve my pride and let them benefit from my mistakes, the gravest of these stemming from my ignorance of the spiritual side of marriage. Unfortunately, this understanding is usually hidden from us at the time we most need it, and it will remain hidden unless we search for it.

Retracing the steps that led to our failures is always uncomfortable, but it is in our best interests (and those of God) when we prayerfully undertake the understanding that can prevent us from repeating those failures.

I grew up thinking of marriage as a happiness goal, never as a holy transaction whereby a man and a woman became subject to God in the fulfilling of the agreement entered into. And I knew even less about the signature of God on that agreement, about which George Sweazy writes:

There are two institutions on the earth which are not really of the earth at all—the Christian Church and the Christian home. These are divine establishments. They are let down from God out of heaven. They are outposts of another realm. God is present in them as he is present in nothing else on earth. Marriage is a divine order of creation. The Christian home is set on earth to be a school for heaven.[1]

God created us to love, and one of the means by which we experience love is through the gift of marriage; however, we must also recognize—that as with everything else in life—marriage was never intended for our benefit alone. This is another case of *what's in it for God!*

Insight does us no good unless we apply it. What gets in our way are the romantic opinions we have been forming since we were very young. We fall in and out of love many times before we finally take our wedding vows, and we make this decision based on our emotions, our relationship with our fathers, and our opinions of ourselves, along with our stockpile of romantic impressions gathered from music, movies, and the books we read.

By the time we are old enough to think about getting married, we have already formed these love opinions, or we should say, love ILLUSIONS. We dream of love, plan for love, wait for love to find us, or go looking for it, but no matter how much we *think* we know about love, we are never ready for the demands love is going to make on us after marriage. We get a healthy dose of reality from Mike Mason in this regard.

Love convinces a couple that they are the greatest romance that has ever been, that no two people have ever loved as they do, and that they will sacrifice absolutely anything to be together. And then marriage asks them to prove it. Marriage is a down-to-earth dimension of romance, the translation of a romantic blueprint into costly reality. It is the practical working out of people's grandest dreams and ideas and promises in the realm of love. It is one of God's most powerful secret weapons for revolutionizing the human heart. It is a heavy, concentrated barrage upon the place of our greatest weakness, which is our relationship with others.[2]

Marriage often gives us a lot more than we ever bargained for, and much less than we anticipated, and we can never be fully prepared for it. Being in love will never sustain a marriage because love, to be love, must meet certain requirements. Among these requirements: that a man and a woman be *capable of* and *willing to* give and receive love from one another for a lifetime. And not everyone is. Love makes beggars of us all in that each of us wants and needs to be loved; not everyone is prepared to give what it takes to make love work.

Unless the initial glow of being *in* love matures into the persevering love of commitment, we will never give what love requires or benefit from what love has to offer. To love and be loved is the most misunderstood and the most sought-after human experience; and we should not be surprised, for love is the pattern whereby we are made in the image of God. It is by love that God reaches man, and by this same love (His love) that we are able to reach others.

We are not born loving. We learn to love. Being made in the image of God gives us a great capacity for love. The human birth defect known as sin gives us an equal capacity to be unloving. Love will always prove itself by the evidence it bears of itself within a relationship. The real proof of love is not how we feel, but how we act. *Love is as love does!* This is true of the love we have for each other and our love of God, and our response to God will tell in our human relationships, as will our indifference to Him. The more we attend to our relationship with Christ, the better marriage partner we become. The more we love God, the more we will cherish each other.

A MYSTICAL UNION

The traditional Christian wedding ceremony defines marriage as a holy, honorable estate, instituted of God, *signifying the mystical union between Christ and his Church* . . . not to be entered into unadvisedly or lightly, but reverently, discreetly, advisedly, soberly, and in the fear of God, both parties agreeing to have and to hold from this day forward, for better for worse, for richer for poorer, in sickness and in health, to love and to cherish, until death, in accordance with God's holy ordinance, including the forsaking of all others.

The sanctity God assigns to marriage makes our love choice all the more crucial, for we are to be subject to one another out of reverence for Christ, Who is spiritually joined with the bride and groom in holy matrimony (Eph. 5:21). The following comments from Dr. Everett J. Worthington Jr. lay down some sobering truth concerning the choice of a spouse.

> When people marry, they unite . . . Their spirits are inextricably joined before God and with God into a three-fold cord (Eccles. 4:9–12) so that their spiritual lives affect each other in ways we cannot understand.[3]

> The joining is so intimate that it is usually referred to in Scripture as becoming one flesh (Gen. 2:24; Matt. 19:5; 1 Cor. 6:16; Eph. 5:31). This implies that the needs of one partner are linked without differentiation to the needs of the other. What hurts or damages one, affects the other. What nourishes one, nourishes the other.[4]

With this in mind, obviously the best way to know the right man is by his relationship with Jesus Christ. Does he have one? To ignore the warning that we not be unequally yoked with unbelievers is to invite misery (2 Cor. 6:14). The Amplified Bible reads, "Do not make mismated alliances with them or come under a different yoke with them, inconsistent with your faith." A man committed to Christ is more likely to be committed to his wife and children. A common faith, like common values and goals, makes living in harmony possible. Indifference to God on the part of even one of the parties puts a marriage in jeopardy. There is much to consider when deciding on a marriage partner, but for the Christian this is not an option. It does not, however, give a Christian grounds to dissolve an already existing marriage, but it does offer the believing spouse the opportunity to partner with God to bring the unbelieving spouse to Christ.

One young couple, married less than a year, sought counseling upon the advice of a concerned relative and were advised to get involved in a church, join a young couples group, and to start praying and reading the Bible together daily. Within weeks their marriage took a turn for the better. What made the difference is that they are equally yoked in their faith in Christ and willing to follow the Christian guidelines that will protect and strengthen their relationship as husband and wife.

LOOKING FOR MR. WONDERFUL

Being chosen by that special man has always been one of the most significant moments in a woman's life. Being chosen is also part of our emotional DNA. The fear of being overlooked is what women of my generation were most concerned with. What if I never get asked the big question? And I don't see any evidence that things have changed. Some of us made poor decisions, saying yes when we should have said no, because being chosen was more important to us at the time than a wise decision.

In my generation it was considered an embarrassment not to be married by the time you were 25. You became the brunt of old-maid jokes. People started asking questions: "Whatever happened to so and so?" "Do you ever see what's-his-name anymore?" The implication was, if you weren't married or engaged, it was because you weren't as desirable as the other girls.

We have always been in search of Mr. Wonderful, the man (we are sure) who holds the key to our happiness. What a woman fears most is: not being chosen, being replaced, and being forgotten, depending upon what stage in the romance cycle she happens to be. Our self-image is so strongly connected to the need to be chosen and paired off that some of us have confused falling in love with falling in NEED.

My first proposal came when I was 19. First I said yes. Then I said no. Maybe we should wait. He pleaded. Soon the lure of belonging and being loved took command of any sensibility; the longings of a lifetime now within my grasp outweighed the occasions when he drank a little too much. All men drank. There was only one thing to consider: he loved me. Now I could tell the world that there was nothing wrong with me after all. And I had the ring to prove it!

Not a good reason to get married, but this is exactly how it happened. I was not the first woman to make this decision based on father-loss, or to trade good sense for pipe dreams, thinking I could change him. So I married a carbon copy of my father: a good-looking ladies' man with a drinking problem and a temper, and the outcome would be for me what it was for my mother, except that I didn't commit suicide over it the way she did. Six years later I married a man of high aspirations and made another mistake—I made him my god!

RISKY BUSINESS

In loving we take the biggest risk of all. Love has the power to either destroy or fulfill us, because to love is to change, to be either more or less than we used to be. To love is to give ourselves to another with no guarantee of the outcome. It is truly a "for better or for worse" condition.

> To love at all is to be vulnerable. Love anything, and your heart will certainly be broken. If you want to make sure to keep it intact, you must give your heart to no one, not even to an animal. Wrap it carefully round with hobbies and little luxuries; avoid all the entanglements; lock it up safe in the casket or coffin of your selfishness. But in that casket—safe, dark, motionless, airless—it will change. It will not be broken; it will become unbreakable, impenetrable, irredeemable. The alternative to tragedy, or at least to the risk of tragedy, is damnation. The only place outside Heaven where you can be perfectly safe from all the dangers of love is Hell.[5]
>
> —C. S. Lewis.

A good marriage doesn't just happen, nor does a bad one. There are many factors at work in both the natural and the supernatural realm, and many of us dive into marriage without knowing what it takes to sustain a marriage. Deciding on the right man, of course, boils down to deciding on a particular man: the one who proposed. And feelings always come first. The hasty heart does not make wise decisions, nor does the heart regulated solely by feelings. Remember, when you marry a man you marry his character.

I spoke to a woman whose fiancé refused to attend premarital classes offered at her church. She was so afraid of losing him that she had agreed to proceed with the wedding as planned in spite of

several warning signs that shouted for a longer engagement period. I told her it would be better to lose him now than five years
and two children later, but in her case, it was too late for advice. I
also remember the woman who was counting the days until her
boyfriend was released from prison. He was a good person at
heart; he'd just had some bad breaks. It didn't matter that he was
given to violent outbursts of temper and addicted to drugs. She
was sure that marriage would make a new man out of him. Both
these women were like the pilot who takes off without a flight
check. Is there enough fuel to complete the flight? Will either of
these marriages be able to go the distance?

THE REAL THING

What I observed of love during my formative years was people hiding behind a pretense of love to get what they wanted. Love came
and went with a person's moods—first it seduced you, then it
turned on you. Love was conditional on my doing the right thing.
Hearing that God was love only put me on the defensive. I saw the
judgment of God not as a manifestation of divine justice, but of
anger, and estimated His opinion of me by my circumstances.

I wanted a safe place that would offset what people did to each
other, a sympathetic God Who encouraged and enabled, and after
years of seeking, that is precisely what I found. But it is not ALL I
found, because love must walk hand-in-hand with justice and deal
with the evil that tries to destroy it, or it cannot claim to be love.
The *anything goes* mentality finds no place with God (Romans
11:22). In the words of Thomas Trevethan, "To stress kindness
without sternness results in the worship of a magnified image of
human tolerance. Sternness without kindness distorts God . . . in
either case we are deprived of that true knowledge of God and of
ourselves which leads to life."[6]

✠

How do we come to a place where we can honestly say we love God? How does it happen? I can't remember a specific day when I suddenly loved Him, just that I gradually came to love Him. "No one can [really] say Jesus is [my] Lord, except by *and* under the power *and* influence of the Holy Spirit" (1 Cor. 12:3). It is only because God first loved us that we can come to love Him.

In creating us in His image, God created in us a need for love. While we pursue love for ourselves, we must not forget that God also desires love. The search of the human heart for authentic love is the echo of the heart of God Who longs to be chosen and cherished by a people who will reverence the depths of His love for *them*.

In commanding us to love Him in return, God turns us in the direction of our greatest need, because if we miss this, we miss everything! For within this commandment is a proposal of love of such intensity that it gives itself to the death rather than see the beloved carried off by another. Christ, like a prince in search of a love of His own, comes to deliver the human race because His heart was pledged to us from before He spoke the world into existence.

Who is this God Who will not share my love with another?

A jealous God.

A God Who loves with such a passion it demanded His life!

And now He asks for mine.

But who is this who comes upon the scene?

Another prince?

He, too, seeks my hand and my life.

"Come away with me, he whispers."

And all of heaven waits to see who I will choose.

To which one will I be joined?

The Prince of Peace or the prince of deception?

Choose wisely, O my soul.

This union is forever.

Confessing our faith in Christ is a more far-reaching decision than we are aware of in the beginning. We don't know enough about God at the time to understand the vision He has for us. He is preparing a people who are not only called by His name, but who will commit to His name. He desires loyalty and unconditional faith equal to His unconditional love. He longs to see the burden of souls, as Murray put it, "that urged Him to Calvary" now urge us to be used in the spreading of the Gospel. He is looking for disciples who will finish the race and not grow weary in well doing. But relax! He doesn't expect us to do it in our own strength—none of us could—yet we must not hesitate to say this is our God and He desires something of us!

Surrendering to Christ doesn't mean a bed of roses. As surely as we can count on a "morning after" in marriage, there will be one in our spiritual union with Christ, because God does not always respond to us in the way we would like. What we can count on is that He will always respond for our eternal good. And He will often use our losses and failures as the very nets to bring us closer to Himself. After we've tried everything else—when we're too weary to put up a fight—then we are snagged. Few of us come to Him as a result of fame and fortune. We are more resistant to His courtship when things are going our way.

Augustine, reflecting on how God worked in his life when he cared nothing for Him, remembered it this way:

> You called me and cried to me and broke open my deafness; You sent Your shafts of light to shine on me and

chase away my blindness; You breathed your fragrant breath on me, and I took a breath and now pant for You; I tasted You, and now I hunger and thirst for You; You touched me and I have burned for Your peace.

You know you love God when you lose your fear of surrender; when you are willing to decrease that He may increase (John 3:30); when you accept His "proposal" of eternal life and are willing to be constrained by the "terms" of repentance, fidelity, and servanthood. The test of holy love is surrender, first to God, and then to each other. And the divine intention between these unions is that they be lived out in holy harmony to the glory of God.

We don't really know the men we marry until we have lived with them, and even then, the "knowing" period can take years because we are reluctant to face each other without our disguises. But God holds nothing back! His character is spelled out for us in the Word, and the Word was made flesh that we might know Him. The more we know of Him, the more we love Him. The more we love Him, the more we want to live for Him. What passion we lack for God He will supply—ask Him.

PERFECT LOVE

Our Lord said that the greatest commandments are that we love God and each other (Matt. 22:37–40). In the context of the supernatural war into which we are born, it is the commandment to love that the Deceiver will target in the life of the individual. There's a war on! And as with all wars, sacrifices are called for. We are called to give up some things in the interest of the Kingdom, yet we often feel put upon when we read our orders from the Commander in Chief. When asked to be considerate, charitable, loving, and forgiving, we may shut the Book and get our focus back on self. And how often we fail to recognize those closest to us as the ones upon whom God would have us first exercise these loving orders.

The commandment to love and serve God through obedience denotes the mark we are to aim for. The call to obedience is part of God's love vocabulary. He is saying: Set your sights on My standards. Learn to relate properly to Me, and you will relate properly to each other. Respond to Me with love, and I will enable you to respond to each other with love. The remedy for the ailments of the family and the whole of society is found in the love commandments.

What we fail to consider is that in missing the target we hit something else: we afflict and hinder others, ourselves, and sin against God. At the same time, we lend a portion of our ground to Satan, allowing him to sow the seed that can take root and choke out the harvest intended for God—the harvest by which our lives will be tested when we stand before Christ.

> I the Lord search the mind, I try the heart, even to give every man according to his ways, according to the fruit of his doings (Jer. 17:10).

Loving others as ourselves is treating them in the way we want to be treated, by allowing the love of God to operate through us as an outflow of what He has freely given us. What we do comes back to us. What we sow into the lives of others we will reap into our own. *And what we sow into the lives of others always comes to rest on the heart of God.*

The only way we will withstand the attacks on our marriages is to apply the love standards set by the example of Jesus Christ. We will not do it in our strength, but we can do it because *He has promised to be in the doing of it with us.* If it were not possible, He would never have established these love standards in the first place. God is telling us this is the way—walk in it. But the decision is always ours.

No discussion about love is complete without the fruits of the Holy Spirit identified in Galatians 5:22. Dwight L. Moody shows us perfect love in operation:

> Love is . . . the first in that precious cluster of fruit . . .
> All the other eight can be put in the word *love*. Joy is
> love exulting, peace is love in repose, long-suffering is
> love on trial, gentleness is love in society, goodness is
> love in action, faith is love on the battlefield, meekness
> is love at school, and temperance is love in training.[7]

Love brings out the best in us, indifference brings out the worst, rendering us fruitless, with nothing of real value to give and nothing of real value to leave behind. In our search for love and acceptance we must remember that those we expect to meet our needs are searching for the very things we seek. For what is society but a stream of needy people in search of authentic love?

Only by God are we equipped to lay aside those things that masquerade as love and extend ourselves for the sake of love itself. We cannot separate the salvation of our souls from the perfecting work that identifies us by our love—even when the people we love the most don't always respond to us as we would like—which brings us to our next topic.

What do we do when the men in our lives don't live up to our expectations?

What do we do when marriage doesn't turn out to be everything we thought it was going to be?

Notes

1. George Sweazy, *In Holy Marriage* (New York: HarperCollins Publishers, 1966), 8.
2. Mike Mason, *The Mystery of Marriage* (Portland, Ore.: Multnomah Press, 1985), 45, 46.
3. Dr. Everett J. Worthington Jr., *Marriage Counseling,* (Downers Grove, Ill.: InterVarsity Press, 1989), 32.
4. Ibid., 37.
5. Excerpt from THE FOUR LOVES by C. S. Lewis, copyright © 1960 by Helen Joy Lewis and renewed 1988 by Arthur Owen Barfield, reprinted by permission of Harcourt, Inc.
6. Thomas L. Trevethan, *The Beauty of God's Holiness* (Downers Grove, Ill.: Intervarsity Press, 1995), 11.
7. Dwight L. Moody, *Secret Power,* Regal Books, (Ventura, Calif.: Regal Books, 1987), 36. Used by permission.

5

When the Men in Our Lives Don't Live Up to Our Expectations

✠

During the "getting to know you" stage of a romantic relationship, we do what we believe will enhance the relationship. We want Mr. Wonderful to think as highly of us as we do of him, and while we are promoting our best self, he is doing exactly the same thing. Is it any wonder then that we are caught off guard the day we see him for what he is—mere flesh and blood—afflicted with the same frailties and flaws as any other man *and* woman? We wake up one morning and realize that the one on the other side of the bed is somebody we really don't know very well after all.

> Tension begins to build.
> We don't know what to do about it.
> Maybe it will pass.
> Why didn't we see this before?
> How could we have been so blind?
> Because love makes us all a little blind.

There comes a time when every married woman must close the door of unrealistic expectations and face reality, which C. S. Lewis has already done for us.

Being in love is a good thing, but it is not the best thing. . . . You cannot make it the basis of a whole life. It is a noble feeling, but it is still a feeling. No feeling can be relied on to last in its full intensity, or even to last at all . . . [but] ceasing to be "in love" need not mean ceasing to love. Love, in this second sense—love as distinct from being "in love" . . . is a very deep unity maintained by the will and deliberately strengthened by habit. . . . "Being in love" first moved them to promise fidelity: this quieter love enables them to keep the promise. It is on this love that the engine of marriage is run; being in love was the explosion that started it.[1]

I once bought a car from a friend. It was every used-car buyer's dream. Then one day the sun hit the door just right. What was this? A ding in the paint? How did that happen? A closer look showed it to be an old dent that had been repaired and painted over, but once I knew it was there, I noticed it every time I approached the car. It wasn't long before I found a gouge in the upholstery. My car had scars, signs of the wear and tear of the past.

We are a lot like this. Our imperfections are not obvious in the beginning. Only after our marriage has some miles on it do we begin to notice the flaws in each other. Discovering the flaws in my car didn't mean it had lost its value in my eyes, but then my car doesn't talk back to me; it can't hurt or manipulate me. I'm not vulnerable to my car except that it can break down, and in that case, it can be repaired. I'm in control of the car. It doesn't control me.

Marriage is as much about dings and dents as it is anything else, because life leaves its marks on us. And a marriage joins more than a man and a woman. It is the combining of two life dramas, two sets of parents, siblings, and any number of bit players within those dramas. We now have a more complicated drama. As the saying goes, "the plot thickens," and the ones most apt to complicate the new drama are the little boy and girl we used to be, and in many instances, continue to be.

One bride tells of how on the day after her wedding she found wet towels and dirty clothes scattered about the bathroom floor. When she asked her husband if he would please clean up his mess so she could take her shower, he said, "Oh, my mother always took care of that sort of thing for me."

"But I'm not your mother!"

A few days later as she cleaned their apartment for the first time, he ran his finger over the top of a window and pointed a dusty finger, saying, "I think you missed something here."

He was right in saying she had missed something. What she had missed during their courtship was a perfectionist personality that made him a natural critic. This played off her background and triggered her insecurities. She wanted a husband, not another critical parent, but she quickly reverted to her old behavior of "walking on eggs" to keep the peace as she did as a child; it was better than losing favor with her husband the way she had with her father. Her husband brought his own disabilities into the marriage as an only child of a doting but domineering mother and an emotionally distant father. He expected his wife to pick up where his mother left off. She was hoping her husband would soothe the wounds inherited from her father. Both continued to demonstrate the imprinting of the past, and both were disappointed.

From the cradle on up we have been observing the way men and women relate to one another. We learn to be ladies and gentlemen by observing ladies and gentlemen. We learn to appreciate and to respond to each other the same way. If our history is full of negatives and we do not *choose* to replace these models with those God holds out to us through the life of Christ, we will relate negatively to our mates and chart the same course for our children to follow.

No matter what our age, we continue to long for comfort in the *dis*comforting areas of our lives. These longings follow us into marriage. Looking to our spouse as a remedy for past unmet needs leads to more disappointment and sets the stage for conflict. Borrowing from Milton again, we can say that not only does the childhood tell the man, it also tells the woman, *and* the marriage.

The men we love are often scarred by events those closest to them may never be aware of. I've worked with men in a support-group setting. I've had my shoulder soaked by their tears, and my heart pierced by their pain. What is needed is a willingness to acknowledge our mutual disappointments in each other in a spirit of empathy and forgiveness and to look to God to meet the needs we cannot possibly meet for each other.

Clinical psychologist Ken Druck explains what is so often missing in the men we love: "I see many men walking around in midlife with a sense of yearning for things that they can't get from their wives and can't get from their jobs and can't pull from inside themselves . . . what the men are missing is a sense of their own identity . . . a very deep sense of validation that passes from father to son."[2]

With all the talk about the differences between men and women, here we find ourselves sharing the same loss. Haven't we, as women, been striving for our identities? Don't we yearn for *something* we aren't getting from our husbands, our jobs, and can't produce within ourselves? Don't father/daughter relationships play as critical a role in our adult years as do father/son relationships in a man's life?

Those of us with unresolved issues are obligated to seek God's remedy for the sake of our marriages, our children, and the part we are to play in the grand scheme of things. God is waiting with open arms to relieve us of those burdens.

We have created an industry out of our differences so that

what was intended to help us better understand each other often serves to further distance us. Rather than point to our differences, we would do well to examine the ground we have in common: first of all, the ground at the foot of the Cross. Our marriages are not failing because men speak an average of 10,000 words a day as compared to 25,000 for women, or because of any of the other differences we've been focusing on.

Our marriages are failing because we resist the Holy Spirit. Until we are willing to acknowledge *this*, understanding our differences will do little to repair or preserve a marriage. Our differences are God-given. It is only when we are yielded to the Holy Spirit that we learn to appreciate those differences and apply them to serve God and each other as He intended.

The battle of the sexes has long been an accepted way of poking fun at each other, and very few of us can honestly say that we have not contributed our share to the joking majority. We call it teasing or joshing, never sarcasm or ridicule—after all, it's all in fun! And as far as those thin-skinned bleeding hearts, isn't it time they got a sense of humor?

Trying to disguise belittling remarks as harmless teasing does nothing to soften the remarks. None of us can add to our value by chipping away at another. Can't we find humor in things other than our differences and our weaknesses? What must arrest us on the spot is knowing that God requires us to appreciate—not depreciate—those made in His image. The Bible tells us that laughter is good medicine, but habitual sarcasm—all in the interest of "fun," of course—puts a strain on the bond between those God has joined together.

When asked to comment on his upcoming divorce, an American billionaire shrugged and said, "If you have to work at marriage, it isn't worth it." He knows how to make money work for him, but nothing of how to make a marriage work. And no marriage will work unless both partners WORK at the marriage. Anyone thinking of marriage would do well to consider these words from Mike Mason: "Holy matrimony, like other holy orders, was never intended as a comfort station for lazy people. On the contrary, it is a systemic program of deliberate and thorough ongoing self-sacrifice."[3]

Of all the things we ask God for, seldom do we ask Him to mature and restore us in the areas most destructive to our relationships. This means change, and change can be painful. As John R. W. Stott explains:

> Indeed, love and pain appear to be inseparable since our fallenness has not been obliterated by our re-creation through Christ. In marriage there is the pain of adjustment, as the old independent "I" gives way to the new interdependent "we." There is also the pain of vulnerability, as closeness to one another leads to self-exposure, self-exposure to mutual knowledge, and knowledge to the risk of rejection. So husbands and wives should not expect to discover harmony without conflict. . . . The giving of oneself to anybody is a recognition of the worth of the other self . . . because I value the other person so highly that I want to sacrifice myself for his or her self. . . . Now to lose oneself that the other may find his or her self—that is the essence of the gospel of Christ. It is also the essence of the marriage relationship . . . each is seeking to enable the other to become more fully himself and herself within the harmonious complementary of the sexes.[4]

IT TAKES THREE

My husband and I never intended to facilitate the destruction of our marriage, yet after years of living what we *thought* was the Christian life, we remained ignorant of the very things that could have prevented the death of a family. We were married in the church. We recited our vows before the altar and meant every word. Yet neither of us recognized the Lordship of Christ over our union, or that we were to *become subject to one another out of reverence for Him* (Eph. 5:21).

It takes three to make a Christian marriage, the third partner being Christ. We can all profit from the experiences of a 17th-century monk, Brother Lawrence, who found his position as head of the monastery kitchen demanding and monotonous until he learned to practice the presence of Christ in the kitchen with him. Lawrence learned to see everything he did as a ministry to God, no matter how insignificant or tedious the work. If he could find God in the kitchen, we can find God in our marriages. But it takes practice!

The reinstatement of basic good manners would also go a long way to improve the emotional climate in the home—if we would respond to each other as we do to our employer or the friends we value so highly. Consider the impact this would have on the younger members of the family as well. When a child sees parents who are considerate of one another, they understand what is expected of them.

"To relax our manners at home," writes George Sweazy, "implies that the other person is not worth the trouble it takes to be polite. It reveals a lack of respect, a failure to honor. Home is a place where we do not have to put on a show; therefore our domestic manners reveal what we truly are. Those who are truly gallant and considerate reveal it most beautifully in their marriages."5

When we are CAREless about how we treat others, others begin to careLESS for us. Each time we take each other for granted we add another brick to the wall that will eventually separate us. Jesus offers the best marital advice ever given: "So in everything, do to others what you would have them do to you." (see Matt. 7:12 NIV)

> Love does not die easily. It is a living thing. It thrives
> in the face of all life's hazards, save one—neglect.
>
> —James D. Bryden

A marriage is often seen as terminal when it is simply a case of two people not knowing which way to turn, and rather than turn to God, they turn on each other.

The once-terminal marriage described below was given new life as a result of one woman's determination to allow Christ to have His way with her, in spite of 20 stormy and frustrating years of marriage. She made Christ the Lord of her life and her marriage—she stopped trying to change her husband—and she let God change her. Three years later her husband made his own commitment to Christ. Is their marriage perfect? Not yet! But this man is now free of a lifetime of bitterness and violent outbursts of rage, and they are working together with God to continue to improve their relationships with Him and with each other. The change in this marriage verifies what Christian psychiatrist Paul Tournier found to be true:

> I have several times received visits from a religious woman who announced at once that she had not come on her own account, but for her husband. . . . She had noted all his faults, and she described them all to me, at the same time expressing the hope that an inner transformation would free him from them. Interviews of

that kind scarcely ever do any good. But if one day that wife returns, not now on behalf of her husband, but on her own account, having resolved to seek before God to find out what changes are needed in her, that will be much more fruitful.[6]

A wife plays a significant role in the spiritual destiny of her husband. Unfortunately, it is a position many of us do not respect. If we could but grasp the significance of our position as coexecutor of the Father's will on the earth, perhaps we could enjoy and even celebrate this position. Herbert Lockyer said of woman, "She is not only man's helper (Gen. 2:18), but also his complement, and is most essential to the completion of his being . . . wherever Christ is recognized as Savior and His truth is obeyed, woman is esteemed as man's loved companion, confidant and, in many ways, his better half."[7]

Note that it is wherever Christ is recognized as Savior and His truth obeyed that the woman is esteemed. It can also be said that wherever Christ is recognized as Savior and His truth obeyed that a woman has no difficulty in honoring her husband. These words send up a flare as to the cause of so many ailing marriages.

A woman is not always seen as cherishable any more than a man is consistently seen as worthy of respect. But do we fail to honor our Lord because our spouse is not honoring us? Do we stop doing it God's way because our husbands are not operating according to God's order for marriage? Certainly not! This also pertains to those times when the "other" appears unlovable in our eyes.

I'm not suggesting we lump all marital conflict into one category. If a spouse turns abusive, remove yourself from danger and seek Biblically based counseling. But even in these critical situations, we are to continue to treat one another as we would like them to treat us, keeping in mind that *Christian love is not an emotion but a decision.* Acting out of obedience always brings the power of God into the situation. Indifference or rebellion toward God always worsens the situation and opens the door to Satan. I speak from experience in saying that many of us give up too easily, and can identify with the following statement from R. Lufton Hudson concerning divorce.

> I fear we are often holding funerals, call it divorce or dissolution, when the marriage is not really dead. It is asleep or intoxicated with hate and hurt. Or it is in a coma. It would seem to be a gross mistake to bury a marriage or a person as the result of a misdiagnosis.[8]

Before a marriage can be transformed, the partners must be transformed. No prayer, no transformation. It was already too late for my marriage, but we still had to "live" with each other in many respects for the sake of our children. So I learned to pray for my ex-husband the way I could have been praying for him before the death of our marriage, had I known then what I know now.

Where would we be if God dealt with us in the way we deal with each other? If He were not so long-suffering with us? A marriage is a pulpit! And its message is contagious, penetrating the minds of our children to shape the next generation. If we, as sons and daughters who are called by His name, will humble ourselves and pray and seek God's face and turn from our wicked ways . . . (2 Chron. 7:14), we will see the healing of our marriages. *And as the home goes—so goes the nation!*

> Confess to one another therefore your faults (your slips, your false steps, your offenses, your sins) and pray [also] for one another, that you may be healed *and* restored [to a spiritual tone of mind and heart] (James 5:16).

The Bible is a treasury of prayer authored by the Holy Spirit for our benefit. The wise woman will apply these prayers long before the situation calls for them and take seriously her role as intercessor on behalf of her husband. We are called to be a blessing to our husbands, and praying the word of God on their behalf helps us pray objectively for them and our marriages. It is also the best way to inventory our own hearts before we point the finger at our mate. When we ask God to bring about the same measure of conviction and correction in us that we desire to see in our spouse, we put ourselves in the very center of His will.

Any Christian who is contemplating divorce would do well to seriously consider the following advice offered by George Sweazy.

> All who see no way except divorce should first seek all the help that a church . . . loving friends, and qualified counselors can give. Let them think deeply about the meanings of Christian love and Christian marriage. Let them ask whether they have used all the help that God has promised, including prayer together. Let them have a time when they quit their accusations and instead admit their faults. Let them make fresh attempts to understand each other. Let them discuss new habits they might try and concessions they might make. Let them know that many a couple has gone through the long-drawn-out agony of a marriage crisis and come out of it into the wonder of a happiness that they never could have guessed was possible.[9]

If you were to ask me to give you a reason for the collapse of my marriage, I would send you to the words of our beloved Savior:

> For everyone who comes to Me and listens to My words [in order to heed their teaching] and does them, I will show you what he is like: he is like a man building a

house, who dug and went down deep and laid a foundation upon the rock: and when a flood arose, the torrent broke against that house and could not shake *or* move it, because it had been securely built *or founded on a rock*. But he who merely hears and does not practice doing My words is like a man who built a house on the ground without a foundation, against which the torrent burst, and immediately it collapsed *and* fell, and the breaking *and* ruin of the house was great (Luke 6:47-49).

True love is not something we find. True love is the fruit of commitment and forgiveness in response to the One who came to live out true love and forgiveness before us.

Notes

1. MERE CHRISTIANITY by C. S. Lewis copyright © C. S. Lewis Pte. Ltd., 1942, 1943, 1944, 1952. Extract reprinted by permission.
2. Paul Ciottie, How Fathers Figure, *Los Angeles Times Magazine*, 18 June18 1989. Copyright 1989, *Los Angeles Times*. Reprinted by permission.
3. Mike Mason, *The Mystery of Marriage* (Portland, Ore.: Multnomah Press, 1985), 138.
4. John R. W. Stott, *God's New Society* (Downers Grove, Ill.: InterVarsity Press, 1980), 236.
5. George Sweazy, *In Holy Marriage,* (New York: HarperCollins Publishers, 1966), 65.
6. Paul Tournier, *The Person Reborn* (New York: HarperCollins Publishers, 1966), 127–128.
7. Herbert Lockyer, *All the Women of the Bible* (Grand Rapids, Mich.: Zondervan Publishing, 1995), 13.
8. R. Lofton Hudson, *Is This Divorce Really Necessary?* (Nashville, Tenn.: Broadman Press, 1983), 169. Used by permission.
9. Sweazy, *In Holy Marriage,* 101.

6

Praying for Men

✠

A married couple has been compared to a pair of oars, pulling together as they move the boat to a prescribed destination. What can we do when two people find themselves rowing in opposite directions? First of all, we turn to God.

What a change we would see in our families if we would pray, and keep on praying, that God restore our husbands to the office of priest of the home. If we would ask, and keep on asking, for the same conviction and correction in our lives as it pertains to the office appointed to us as his helpmate. If we would ask God to reveal to us those things in us which undermine our relationships with each other.

> Search me [thoroughly], O God, and know my heart!
> Try me and know my thoughts! And see if there is any
> wicked *or* hurtful way in me, and lead me in the way
> everlasting (Ps. 139:23–24).

Do not attempt to pray for your spouse in resentment or as one who holds a grudge. The Lord will not hear you if you approach Him this way (Ps. 66:18). Pray first of all that His perfect will be brought to bear in your relationship with your husband, applying the Scripture to what you are asking God to do for you.

Proverbs 21:1 "The King's heart is in the hand of the Lord, as are the watercourses; He turns it whichever way He wills."

Acknowledge that your husband's heart is in the hand of God. Pray that God turns the heart of the man you love to follow the ways of God and to turn your heart as well, so that as one flesh you will both go the way of God.

Ezekiel 36:26-27 "A new heart I will give you and a new spirit will I put within you, and I will take away the stony heart out of your flesh and give you a heart of flesh. And I will put my Spirit within you and cause you to walk in My statues, and you shall heed My ordinances and do them." Personalize this Scripture by asking God to first work on the attitude of *your* heart, and by His Spirit move you to follow Him. Then pray in this manner on behalf of your husband.

Psalm 51:10 "Create in me a clean heart, O God, and renew a right, persevering, *and* steadfast spirit within me." Pray this for yourself, then your husband, then the two of you together. This is the first prayer I plan to teach my grandsons. I want these words written on their hearts to help them avoid the pitfalls their grandfather and I were not equipped to avoid because we never approached God this way.

We are to pray for those who hurt us—Jesus tells us to pray for them—not because we feel like it—but in obedience in order that God's plan will be accomplished in our relationships. Obedience in this one area alone will change your heart. And a heart change in you will affect others around you in the same way a ripple in a pond displaces the water around it. Ask God to instill in you His love for the man you pray for. Pray that your husband gets a sense of his value to God, then you put this same value on your husband. Pray not so much for a change in him to make your life easier, but to bring about God's will for the one you pray for.

Marital wounds cut deep. Respect and trust are priceless bonds between a man and a woman, and once broken, take time and commitment to restore. Our Lord asks us to turn our grievances into prayer: for the eternal sake of those who have grieved us, for our sake, and for His sake. I didn't have this understanding when my marriage was failing. I couldn't pray God's heart for my husband or myself. I didn't know God's heart because I didn't know the Scriptures.

The attitudes and opinions handed down through the generations are certain to show up in your marriage, so don't be surprised. If you witnessed love and mutual respect among family members, these strengths will reinforce your adult relationships. And if this is the case, I trust you remember to continually thank God for such a blessing. My husband and I did not share such a heritage. He imitated his father, following the same unhealthy model set by his parents in the way they interacted with each other. I reacted out of my history. And neither of us understood what was happening. Our marriage perished for a lack of knowledge of God and for a lack of the vision of marriage from God's perspective.

Satan is on to us. He is out to destroy the sanctity of marriage, using our attitudes toward each other as ammunition aimed at our own households. James 4:7–8 shows us how to defend ourselves: "So give yourselves humbly to God. Resist the devil, and he will flee from you. And when you draw close to God, God will draw close to you." (TLB) We can't apply the second portion of this passage until we have responded to the first. Again, the key is that we submit ourselves to God—that we order our lives according to His will.

THE BIBLICAL REMEDY

The following Scriptures map out the way God would have us go when our marriages are in trouble:

> Never return evil for evil or insult for insult (scolding, tongue-lashing, berating), but on the contrary blessing [praying for their welfare, happiness, and protection,

and truly pitying and loving them]. For *know that* to this you have been called, that you may yourselves inherit a blessing [from God—that you may obtain a blessing as heirs, bringing welfare and happiness and protection] (1 Peter 3:9).

For the eyes of the Lord are upon the righteous (those who are upright and in right standing with God) and His ears are attentive to their prayer. But the face of the Lord is against those who practice evil [to oppose them, to frustrate and defeat them] (1 Peter 3:12).

In 2 Corinthians 10:5 we are taught to demolish arguments and take our thoughts captive to make them obedient to Christ. How easily *we* are taken captive by our thoughts—by those attitudes and arguments we rehearse in our minds—which then spring into action and do harm to ourselves and others. We *can* intercept our thoughts before we say or do something we'll regret, before our words become the very club that beats a marriage to death.

This also applies to airing your grievances with anyone who will listen. When you hold your husband up to criticism before others, you will elicit all manner of advice that is in direct opposition to what God wants to do in answer to your prayers. When you dishonor your husband before others, you also dishonor the Lord Who is the third member of the marriage.

And what this love consists in is this: that we live *and* walk in accordance with *and* guided by His commandments (His orders, ordinances, precepts, teaching). This is the commandment, as you have heard from the beginning, that you continue to walk in love [guided by it and following it] (2 John 1:6).

We are to have the same loving attitude toward each other as Christ has toward us. It is this very attitude that we find expressed in Romans 15:5–7:

> Now may the God Who gives the power of patient endurance (steadfastness) and Who supplies encouragement, grant you to live in such mutual harmony *and* such full sympathy with one another, in accord with Christ Jesus, that together you may [unanimously] with united hearts *and* one voice, praise and glorify the God and Father of our Lord Jesus Christ (the Messiah). Welcome *and* receive [to your hearts] one another, then, even as Christ has welcomed *and* received you, for the glory of God.

The Living Bible translation of verse 5 reads:

> May God Who gives patience, steadiness, and encouragement help you to live in complete harmony with each other—each with the attitude of Christ toward the other.

Husbands and fathers are responsible to God for the positions given them as priest of the Christian home. However, God did not appoint us as judge, but as helpmate, and when we get out of line with God's purposes we start working for the enemy. We cannot abdicate *our* God-appointed position because our husbands are not always what we would like them to be or all that God calls them to be.

The tension between what God asks of us and what we think we can give Him is enormous when it comes to marital conflict. We don't arrive at this overnight. But we will never do it at all unless we commit to the process as it is revealed through the teachings of Jesus Christ, and we cannot do that until we first make a commitment to the Teacher.

> Obedience changes the situation because it brings into the situation a power accessible only through obedience.

This is the most effective weapon we have in the defense of our marriages. We must first tend to our own relationship with God and stop trying to change our husbands. Only God can do that. No woman can "fix" what she perceives to be wrong with the man she married.

DAUGHTERS OF GRACE

Grace is most often defined as God's unmerited favor. Included in the definition of grace listed in Strong's Concordance of the Bible is the *divine influence upon the heart and its reflection in the life.*[1] It is this influence that enables us to obey, and it will be from this same influence that the men we love, as well as our children, will see Jesus reflected in our lives. Our part is to make the decision to participate in the life-enabling power known as the grace of God.

> Laboring together [as God's fellow workers] with Him then, we beg of you not to receive the grace of God in vain [that merciful kindness by which God exerts His holy influence on souls and turns them to Christ, keeping and strengthening them—do not receive it to no purpose] (2 Cor. 6:1).

If our lives are to count for anything when they are weighed, let it be for this: that we chose obedience, for this is what pleases our Lord. When what matters to Him is what matters to us, then obedience becomes more visible in our lives. Habits are made and broken the same way—by repetition. This is not to say we won't stumble, because we will. But God is faithful to complete the work in us if we choose to go His way and not our own.

We must decide to cooperate with God. This is enough to change us, our husbands, our children, and yes, even eternity. When the hand that rocks the cradle is empowered through obedience, both heaven and earth will benefit.

> Obedience is a particular means of joy and the only means of that particular joy.

> —Charles Williams

MAKING PEACE WITH OUR FATHERS

We want to see our fathers as the hero when in reality they may be so plagued by the fallout of their life experiences that they are incapable of meeting the needs of those given into their care. Sometimes a man's reputation is more important to him than the needs of his family. If a man is controlled by alcohol or drugs, he cannot fill a hero's shoes. Our fathers may have done all manner of physical and emotional damage to us, but God desires that we make peace with them so that we, ourselves, can live in peace. Unforgiven family wounds can make us physically *and* emotionally ill.

I can only speculate as to why my father abandoned me. We know that when an individual is not submitted to the Holy Spirit, they are manipulated by ungodly spirits with all manner of unfortunate outcomes. I found peace by forgiving my father and praying that he be delivered from alcoholism. It is by choice that the peace process begins, and through Christ the Mediator, that peace is attained and maintained.

Godly choices are backed by the power of God so that the decision of the mind leads to the authentic forgiveness of the heart. Forgiveness, like love, is a decision, not a feeling. The heart need not be involved in the decision-making process in the beginning; however, once the decision is made and acted on, the heart decision will follow.

Beyond the effects our prayers have on others, prayer affects us and our fellowship with God. More will be said about this aspect of prayer in a subsequent chapter, but as it relates to making peace with our fathers—or anyone else—God must be involved in the process with us. As the Holy Spirit first prepared our hearts to partake of the gift of salvation, He alone can work in us the capacity to forgive the family wounds.

So we pray: Lord, I choose to forgive.
Lord, help my unforgiveness.

When I first began to deal with the issue of forgiveness, I was uncomfortably aware that forgiveness came cheap when I wanted it for myself. It carried a far higher price tag when it was my turn to extend it to others. What enabled me to forgive those I found most difficult to forgive was not only recognizing the enormous forgiving love given me, but that God, in the Person of Jesus Christ, was willing to bear the penalty for what I had suffered. I didn't forgive because I was naturally a forgiving person. It was God transforming my old nature so that I was willing to forgive— God working in me the desire to see that those who had violated my body receive their Salvation and be healed of the diseases of their souls.

One day I cried aloud, "Dear God, do you realize I've spent two-thirds of my life paying for other men's crimes?" It was then that the small, still, so recognizable voice spoke to me a second time. "I understand what it means to pay for other men's crimes."

Suddenly forgiveness was no longer an issue; it was a privilege. I was overcome with forgiveness—for His sake—seeing for the first time that Jesus paid for these very same crimes. Prior to this moment, the Cross always represented my sin, my failure, my guilt. I never considered that it was also the sins perpetrated upon me that drove the nails into His sacred body. What had happened to me was of such consequence that the Father demanded payment for my wounds, and only a Person of great worth could pay the price.

Now I saw how the Father also shared in my suffering to the extent of the death of His only Son. Would I wound Him further by not accepting the sacrifice and the love that provided it? It was an awareness and compassion for the heart of God that relieved me of the anger and brokenness over wasted years, and I could forgive not the acts themselves, but those who committed them.[2]

Forgiveness is an attitude developed in us through the conforming work of the Holy Spirit. We cannot in our own strength maintain a life of forgiveness. Of course, some things are easier to forgive than others, but does God make allowances for degrees of obedience here? No! He says, "Forgive." Certainly, when we pray, *forgive us as we forgive others,* there is an element of the principle *do unto others as you would have others do unto you*—most certainly as we would have God do unto us. The best way to squelch any resentment that might surface is to immediately pray for the person and situation associated with those feelings. We are to hate sin (as God hates sin) but not to hate the sinner. Our Lord said, "Pray for them."

Notes

1. *Strong's Exhaustive Concordance of the Bible,* New Testament #5485
2. Donna Ferguson, *The Someday Kid* (Summerland, Calif.: Harbor House (West) Publishers, 1993), 217.

To Forgive

O Jesus,
I choose to forgive
And desire to forget.
But how can I forgive and forget?
For I am blessed and cursed with memory.
His answer came clear:
I will superimpose Myself
Upon that specific of your life
Where you choose to forgive
And desire to forget!

O Jesus,
Superimpose Yourself upon that event
So when I look at it
I see only Jesus;
Superimpose Yourself upon that person
So when I look at her
I see only Jesus;
Superimpose Yourself upon myself
So as I look out
I see only Jesus.
I now see through the Veil of His Person
Which view changes all:
Them and me.

—Nadine Ellis Bennett

7

MOTHERHOOD
FACT AND FICTION

In many respects, motherhood is a role you have to play before you can get the hang of it. I approached it like I did the YWCA swimming pool when I was a girl. I jumped in and paddled for all I was worth until I learned to keep my head above water. I was determined to be the mother I never had and to give my children everything I'd missed out on when I was growing up, never suspecting at the time how unrealistic a goal I'd set for myself.

We cannot help but enter the parenting phase of our lives with the same unreasonable expectations we bring into marriage, looking to our children to fulfill a role God never intended. We are inclined to see a child as an extension of ourselves, made in our image, and given for our happiness—when it is God Who has first rights to our children—something I never took into account when I was raising mine. Nor did I consider that there is an eternal purpose operating between us in the linking of mother to child, or a plan that preempted any I might have.

The mother/child relationship, like the marriage relationship, is for better or for worse, in sickness and in health, and for as long as you both shall live. It can also be said that the secret to successful mothering is the same as that of a successful marriage—to recognize that this relationship is also for Somebody much bigger than the two of you.

To become a mother is to enter into a unique love affair, one that begins long before the beloved is seen, held, or known. Once life is conceived within us, we cannot remain as we were, and God does not intend that we should, for to be with child is to shelter a sacred trust and to minister to God in a most profound way.

If we define conception and birth in biological terms alone, with no regard for the divine engineering and purpose behind the conception of a child, we have an incomplete definition of life. The same is true if we fix the limits of the life of a child as the number of years he or she will spend on earth. Conception is the beginning of a life that will never end. As we consider the worth of a child, we must also take note of his or her potential, of which J. Moorage writes:

> They are the men and women of the future, and within them lurk wondrous possibilities and powers which shall be developed and manifested and felt another day . . . within the soul of every little child in our homes, in our schools, and in our streets, there is a moral force lying hidden on which two ultimately opposite eternities hang.[1]

A HOLY PARTNERSHIP

When a child asks where babies come from, we can honestly say they come from God, for every child was first conceived in His heart before they got to us. He foreknew their names and their days, as well as those of us privileged to carry, birth, and nurture their lives. As a mother, our role is that of a partner in a joint venture whereby an eternal plan is realized.

We want our children to be happy, to reach their full potential, and to accomplish something of significance. So does God, only His vision is not what most of us consider when we begin raising a family. His plan is that the parent guide the child from physical birth (over which the child has no choice) to the second birth of the spirit (over which the child *does* have a choice). Blessed is the woman whose motive is to discover and nourish what lies hidden within her children to prepare them to respond to the cause of Christ.

Our part is to teach a child to choose the right path, so that when he is older he will remain upon it (Prov. 22:6). God has already done His part in giving us the training manual and the promise of His Spirit to guide us, but it takes a woman whose motives are to do the will of God to put into practice what it takes to be a mother in the true sense of the word.

GROWING PAINS

I remember a friend who adopted two children and saw them lured away by the Deceiver. The most difficult day of her life was the day she visited her son in prison for the first time. But today, five years after her death, he and his sister are closer to God than during her lifetime, because the mother He gave them (in place of the mother who could not keep them) remained faithful. She was not governed by her heartbreak, but by what God called her to do. And that was to love them through whatever came along—to let her life speak louder than the words they refused to hear—and to intercede on their behalf.

There is a price to pay for any worthwhile endeavor. The cost of parenting is similar to that of becoming a disciple of Christ in that it also calls for the laying aside of self on behalf of a greater cause and living by faith in anticipation of the future. When the travail of childbirth becomes the travail of parenting, we are apt to cry out to God, "This child YOU have given me." Growing pains are as much a part of a mother's life as they are of a child's, and should the time come, as it inevitably will (except in very rare instances) that God lets them eat the bitter fruit of having their own way, she will partake of the same plate.

Our children are a heritage from the Lord (Ps. 127:3). When we stand beside the bed of a sleeping child, it's easy to thank God for the blessing. But when there isn't enough of us to go around, we don't always see them in that light. Children don't come equipped with off and on switches, so there will be times when we don't feel up to the demands of the job.

One woman told me of her frustration as a single parent and the problems of managing a six-foot-teenager. "Sometimes I see him as my baby, sometimes as my ex-husband, and I want to divorce him. Sometimes he is absolutely precious, and I feel so privileged to be his mother. It's like a roller-coaster ride: sometimes I'm up, sometimes I'm down."

God gets a lot of mileage out of children when it comes to the conforming work of Romans 8:29. They act as chisels, hammers, and sandpaper—as humbling blocks that bring us to our knees time and time again. They challenge us, defy us, and stretch us beyond what we believe to be our limits. Sometimes they are embarrassed to be seen with us. Sometimes they would rather belong to the family next door. And no matter how often we tell them we love them, they are continually questioning our motives.

> Psalm 8:4 asks the question: "What is man that You are mindful of him, and the son of [earthborn] man that You care for him?

> Do you *know* that your children are created to assume a position of responsibility over the works of God (Gen. 1:26)?

Do you *believe*, as God declares in His Word, that your children are created a little lower than the angels (Ps. 8:5)?

Do you *understand* that your children are meant to become an heir of God and a co-heir with Christ (Rom. 8:16–17)?

If these truths have not been planted into your life, I urge you to memorize these Scriptures, asking the Holy Spirit to quicken them to your understanding so that you can teach them to your children. Train them up in the knowledge of who they were created to be. Start today!

TESTING, TESTING

The last thing on our minds when we look into the face of an infant is that this endearing and helpless little creature comes equipped with a built-in parent-resisting will of its own. Some fight us every inch of the way; others are more compliant, but every child will attempt to get the upper hand, at least for the moment, so be prepared. Discipline is not a pleasant duty, but it *is* a duty.

If the Lord disciplines those He loves, so must we (Heb. 12:5–9). But this does not mean that we discipline without understanding and compassion. We can be very clumsy in dealing with our children. When we fail to make time for them, we frustrate them; when we discipline in anger rather than love, we break their spirit.

Do not irritate *and* provoke your children to anger [do not exasperate them to resentment], but rear them [tenderly] in the training *and* discipline *and* the counsel and admonition of the Lord (Eph. 6:4).

When parents are honored God is honored. Obedience carries with it the same blessings for a child as for a parent, and the earlier we plant these concepts into young minds the better it will be for all concerned. Dr. James Dobson stresses the importance of letting our children know the truth regarding a parent's role in the family:

> I cannot overemphasize the importance of instilling two distinct messages within your child before he is forty-eight months of age: (1) "I love you more than you can possibly understand. You are precious to me and I thank God every day that He let me raise you!" (2) "Because I love you, I must teach you to obey me. That is the only way I can take care of you and protect you from things that might hurt you." Let's read what the Bible tells us, "Children, obey your parents, for this is what God wants you to do (Eph. 6:1)."[2]

He also urges us to pray with our children when they seek reassurance after a time of discipline. "It is extremely important to pray with the child at that time, admitting to God that we have *all* sinned and no one is perfect. Divine forgiveness is a marvelous experience, even for a very young child."[3]

Discipline does not produce an unhappy child, as some would have us believe. What most threatens the happiness of a child is the lack of authentic love. The child raised on the law of love established by the One Who created him or her is best prepared for this life and the next.

> For the time being no discipline brings joy, but seems grievous *and* painful; but afterwards it yields a peaceable fruit of righteousness to those who have been trained by it [a harvest of fruit which consists in righteousness—in conformity to God's will in purpose,

thought, and action, resulting in right living and right standing with God] (Heb. 12:11).

If we do not influence a child's mind for good, a thousand tutors outside the home will influence it to its harm. A child's mind is like a bank: what goes into it comes back years later—with interest. The primary objective in parenting is the good of the child; therefore, it becomes our duty to train up the child to yield to the will of God. And we cannot do this unless we are trained up ourselves.

> And these words which I am commanding you this day shall be [first] in your *own* minds *and* hearts; [then] you shall whet and sharpen them so as to make them penetrate, *and* teach *and* impress them diligently upon the [minds and] hearts of your children. . . . (Deut. 6:6).

It is sobering to think that our influence reaches beyond the boundaries of our homes and lifetimes because of what we are investing in the next generation. And if that doesn't humble us, nothing will! In the midst of these revelations, we see the importance of adhering to the narrow way that leads to the Kingdom of God, for our children are only a step behind.

One day my daughters came to me complaining that they never had a say in what went on in the family. I explained that the family operated like a kingdom with Daddy as King, Mommy as Queen, and the two of them as princesses. The King and Queen decided what was best for everyone because they had all the responsibility. When they became parents, they could make the decisions. I also told them that their children wouldn't like the arrangement any better than they did, but that was just the way it was.

As effective as this example was at the time, I regret having left out the most important Person in the family. Children need to be taught that it is God Who assigns parents their position within the family unit. And as children are to honor and obey the parents, parents are required to honor and obey God in carrying out their duties to Him as the Sovereign head of the family and as guardians of the children He has given them.

For a Lifetime

Seldom do our children turn out the way we anticipated or take the road we envisioned for them. Sometimes, no matter what we do, they stray into the Deceiver's camp and choose to live there. We think back to the initial joy of holding them in our arms for the first time and wonder what went wrong? What could we have done differently?

Put yourself in this word picture: You are walking down the corridor of a hospital maternity ward. The delivery room doors swing open. In the center of the room a doctor and his attending staff prepare to receive a child into the world. Unseen by anyone except you are two large figures at opposite sides of the room. As the birth becomes imminent, the two figures step forward. You recognize that these are angels, and that only one has come to protect. The other is of a different kingdom. His purpose is to destroy. At the infant's first cry, swords are drawn—and the battle is on!

What we have here is a custody battle as a result of the introduction of sin into the plan of God. Although God has legal custody of all children through the atoning life and death of Christ, they are the ones who will ultimately choose who they will make their eternal home with. There is no such thing as joint custody in the spiritual realm. What makes motherhood so holy a calling is what is at stake within the relationship—that is, the welfare of an individual created by God, entrusted to us for a lifetime. Yes, a lifetime! We are to be spiritually involved in the welfare of our children through example, love, and intercession for as long as we live.

Larry Christenson writes, "When God finds parents who are willing to take time apart for prayer, he is going to have families through whom He can work . . . Jesus' presence in the family will become real to the children because it is real to you."[4] Knowing what I know now, there is no doubt that my children were hindered because I was not aware of the critical difference a praying parent can make. But as one friend speaking from her own experience told me, "You did the best you could, at the time, under the circumstances, with the light you had."

My best at the time was to recite the Lord's Prayer with them, supervise bedtime prayers, insist they take turns saying grace at mealtimes, and see that they attended Sunday school regularly. I prayed that I would be here for as long as they needed me and that they would escape the hardships of my childhood. But I never saw my responsibility to pray for their relationship with Christ *and* that His perfect will be accomplished in their lives.

What a role model we have in the life of Kathleen Thomas Stewart, who went daily to an unused garage she called the Prayer House where her children could hear her praying for them by name. Dr. Mary Stewart Relfe gives the following account of her mother's prayer habits:

> As far back as memory serves me, days at our house began and ended with my mother conducting Family Altar. She would read a portion of Scripture and follow it with an application, as it related to our conduct and character. All of us would then kneel for prayer. From the oldest child, in order of descending ages, each

would pray individually. The youngest was instructed in prayer until it became a status symbol to be old enough to pray one's own prayers at about age four.[5]

Begin praying for your children the very moment you know that you are *with child.* Let them hear the name of Jesus spoken over them from the cradle up. When they are old enough to understand, let them see how God is consulted in the daily affairs of the family. Let them experience the life of the church. Talk about how they can get involved in what God is doing in the world *through* the church. Encourage them to participate in activities that will *draw* them rather than coerce them to God. And remember, a relationship with Christ will not be important to the child if it is not important to the mother.

Let us determine to parent according to the will of God and then depend upon the Holy Spirit to bring our children to His desired end. The Holy Spirit enables us to face the unfaceable, do the undoable, and bear the unbearable. While parenting may present all of these challenges, we can be assured that He will be parenting *us* as we parent our children.

But what do we do when our own flesh and blood betrays us, when a son or daughter says, "Your God will not be my God?" We remember that the Lord knows our seed and marks them for the promise: "I will contend with those who contend with you and I will save your children" (Isa. 49:25). If we will yield to the influence of the Holy Spirit, though our children may rebel and choose to explore the other kingdom, like the prodigal, they will return to the Kingdom of God (see Luke 15:11–32).

For the same reason that the Apostle Paul prayed for the early church, we can come to God on behalf of our children and ask that He grant our children the mighty inner strengthening of His Spirit . . . that Christ be more and more at home in their hearts, living within them as they trust in Him . . . that the roots of their souls go down deep into the soil of His marvelous love . . . that they will know how long, how wide, how deep, and how high His love really is, and to experience this love for themselves (see Eph. 3:14–19, TLB).

THE EMPTY CRIB

What do we say to the woman who remains childless, not by choice but by circumstance? What will comfort the longing of her heart? I would not presume to understand her longing, because I have borne and raised children. However, I have learned that God does not always satisfy our present longings but redirects them into the stream of His compassion to meet a need elsewhere.

If you are childless, are you willing to invest your longing for a child into a child who needs encouragement? What about becoming prayerfully involved in the lives of those who pass your home on their way to school every day? Consider the children who may not have praying parents and the difference your prayers can make. Women are meeting regularly for the sole purpose of praying for children. They also get together to pray over the telephone. Many of them have no children of their own, but through prayer they participate in the eternal destiny of those they may never meet this side of heaven.

A picture of a six-year-old boy who was attending a summer camp for underprivileged children appeared in our local newspaper recently. There he was in a strongman pose, straining for all he was worth to show his muscles, with the most menacing expression he could muster, for a six-year-old, that is. I was overcome with sadness for this child. One has to wonder what his picture will look like a year from now—20 years from now—and who will pray for him?

There is no end to the opportunities to partner with God on

behalf of children. Watch the evening news and you will find a child to pray for. Interceding for children can become a profitable holy habit for us and for God.

> Whosoever receives one of these little ones in
> My name receives Me (Matt. 18:5).

MOTHERS AND DAUGHTERS

There is a door of understanding between a mother and a daughter that only a grandchild can open. I remember having a sense of connectedness and respect bordering on awe for mothers everywhere after becoming a mother myself, and witnessed an identical discovery in my daughters after the birth of their children.

One of my fondest memories is that of my eldest daughter cradling her newborn son in her arms and looking at me as if she had just seen me for the first time. "Mom, when I was growing up I used to think, what's the big deal about being a mother? How hard can it be to raise kids? Now I'm wondering how you did it." I also cherish the day my youngest daughter said, "Please take care of yourself, Mom—I want you to be around to pass on your wisdom to my son when he is older." I also remember a time when my views were judged as old-fashioned and irrelevant!

Appreciation from one's own flesh and blood ranks at the top of any mother's list. Missing it can be one of her greatest sorrows. The same is true when we fail to appreciate the differences in our children or forget that growing up is as challenging for them—if not more so—as it was for us.

I have traveled both sides, as a child in need of a mother, and as a mother who wanted to give her children more than she was capable of providing. There is as great a need to make peace with our mothers as with our fathers. Surely this also carries the imprint of *do to others as you would have them do to you.*

One woman wanted to know how she could forgive her mother when she felt nothing but hatred for her. As long as her mind was set in opposition to the will of God, it would be impossible to forgive her mother. Only she and God knew if she was truly *willing* to forgive, but if she was, I suggested she ask God to give her His love for her mother—to give her a change of heart concerning her mother—and to pray *for* her mother. It is important that we talk to God about our feelings and ask Him to give us His love for the person or persons we need to forgive. We become the slaves of those we will not forgive—whether they be alive or dead.

The closer our walk with God, the more we forgive and the more we are able to extend to others what we continually need for ourselves. Those who are peacemakers "will plant seeds of peace and reap a harvest of goodness" (James 3:18, TLB).

We are not going to be able to live up to our children's expectations. They will have their complaints against us. Some with good reason. But to become a parent is to better understand a parent, and it will be the same for them.

Notes

1.   Joseph S. Exell, *The Bible Illustrator, Vol. 2: Matthew 18:14* (Grand Rapids, Mich.: Baker Books, 1977), 405.

2.   *The Strong-Willed Child,* Dr. James Dobson, © 1978 by Tyndale House Publishers, Inc. Used by permission. All rights reserved.

3.   Ibid., 33.

4.   Larry Christenson, *The Christian Family* (Minneapolis, Minn: Bethany Fellowship, 1970), 165.

5.   Dr. Mary Stewart Relfe, *Cure of All Ills* (Montgomery, Ala.: League of Prayer, 1988), 1.

8

THE PERPETUAL BEAUTY CONTEST

✠

In our search for spiritual truth we cannot ignore the physical realities of our existence, and given the fact that one of the most pressing realities for a woman is her physical appearance, we are going to take what may appear to be a spiritual detour for a few paragraphs.

Somerset Maugham strikes a familiar chord in saying that, it goes hard with a woman who fails to adapt herself to the prevalent masculine conception of her. It can go equally as hard with a child who fails to meet the physical expectations of a parent. This touches on a very sensitive issue for many who may be reading this material. The grief of knowing we don't measure up to the physical expectations of others is tremendous.

The emphasis our culture puts on beauty would have us believe that a woman teamed up with an attractive man is made more desirable by reason of association, and a man paired off with a beautiful woman is somehow more of a man. The truth is that we have all looked to others to enhance our self-image.

Our beauty consciousness is awakened the moment we hear *what a pretty little girl* directed at someone other than ourselves. Long before we begin primping in front of Mommy's mirror, we see ourselves through the eyes of those most important to us, particularly our fathers, and if the image reflected in Daddy's eyes is not the one we were looking for—or if Daddy isn't there—our conception of self is distorted. So begins the search for a better self-image.

It is heart-wrenching to see a young girl struggling for her identity. We've all been through it. It doesn't take us long to figure out how we rank alongside the other girls, because we measure ourselves by each other. The competition grows more intense year by year; for many it becomes an endless search for approval and an ongoing source of pain.

To make the most of what we have, we look to the fashion and cosmetic brokers who peddle a look that for many of us is unattainable. But that doesn't stop us from buying the magazines and wondering, *If I buy this product, can I really look like her?* We think that the more closely we resemble the beautiful people, the easier life will be, because in the real world beauty counts. And unless we were taught it beforehand, we don't know that beauty counts as much in the spiritual realm as it does in the physical realm, but for entirely different reasons.

In His Image

If, in our search for a better self-image, we will seek the God in Whose image we are made, we can reclaim our legitimate stature and escape the competition-and-comparison trap. And to do this, we go back to the very beginning when God said, *"Let Us make man in Our image, after Our Likeness"* (Gen. 1:26).

You and I perceive each other with our natural senses, but there is also something supernatural about us that is above and beyond what we are naturally aware of. It is unfortunate that the supernatural is most often consigned to psychic phenomena and science fiction, for it is to the supernatural realm that the hidden self belongs. The body is the outer structure by which we are recognized in the physical or natural world. But more remarkable than this outer structure and the complex biological systems that support it is the component of self known as spirit, which allows us to relate to God like no other created being, including the angels.

We bear a physical resemblance to our parents. We also bear a spiritual resemblance by way of a spirit-nature to God, which must also experience birth, as Jesus said, "from above" before it is capable of responding to the One Who created it (John 3:3–6). Matthew Henry defines the spirit as "the inner chamber in the believer where the Holy Spirit has taken possession and carries out His work of making the soul and body holy unto the Lord."[1] It is also where we find the beautiful image so valuable to God.

> Let not yours be the [merely] external adorning with [elaborate] interweaving *and* knotting of the hair, the wearing of jewelry, or changes of clothes; but let it be the inward adorning *and* beauty of the hidden person of the heart, with the incorruptible *and* unfading charm of a gentle and peaceful spirit, which [is not anxious, or wrought up, but] is very precious in the sight of God. (1 Peter 3:3–4).

MORE THAN MEETS THE EYE

The amount of time spent in the preparation of the self varies from woman to woman, but we all know it takes a great deal of time. Self must be made up, dressed up, and accessorized so self can step out into the world. But what the world sees is not the real me—the image you work so hard to perfect is not the real you. No matter how we describe ourselves or how we appear to others, our true identity is hidden beneath the wrappings of the flesh and known only to God.

We are made in the image of God. God is Spirit. We are spirit! It is the spirit of a woman that God is conforming to fit His eternal purpose. No mirror can reflect the human spirit. The evidence of the spirit can only be seen in the character of an individual.

There was a woman, described as one of the most kindly among leaders of American society, who once saw herself as the only homely girl in a class of exceptionally pretty ones. Then a wise teacher intervened and gave the unhappy girl a lump of coarse earth and instructed her to plant, water, and give it sun for a few weeks. When the girl returned several weeks later with a golden Japanese lily her teacher said, "Who would believe so much beauty and fragrance were shut up in that little, rough, ugly thing?"[2]

The dormant plant required care before it could show itself. The spiritual potential lying dormant in each of us must be nourished by the Word of God before it springs to life. Jesus said, "Man shall not live *and* be upheld *and* sustained by bread alone, but by every word that comes forth from the mouth of God" (Deut. 8:3, Matt. 4:4). It is the Holy Spirit Who alters the disposition and shapes the inner person of the heart with its incorruptible beauty, and He does it through the revelation of His Word.

Is it possible to come to terms with what we see in the mirror if what we see reflected back is less than we would like it to be? The answer is yes! But first we must take another look at ourselves through a mirror capable of penetrating beneath the skin. The competition and the search for identity stops when we look into the Scriptures. Nothing will distort this mirror. We *will* see our blemishes, but we will also discover the beauty potential of the spirit where the truly beautiful woman is formed by the One Who defines beauty at its highest level.

> God did not create the body for exhibition. He created it for Himself.

> Do you not know that your body is the temple (the very
> sanctuary) of the Holy Spirit Who lives within you,
> Whom you have received [as a Gift] from God? You are
> not your own. You were bought with a price [purchased
> with a preciousness and paid for, made His own]. So
> then, honor God *and* bring glory to Him in your body
> (1 Cor. 6:19, 20).

Our bodies are a unique and wonderfully created structure
intended first of all to worship and honor God. They are also a
dispensary for the love of God in a world oppressed by disappointment and human failure, and we, as followers of Christ, are
to bear witness to the remedy for the ailments of humanity.

The next time you pass a magazine rack, notice how many are
dedicated to the adornment and preservation of the body. We are
to respect and care for our bodies, but not to worship our bodies.
And in this regard our first priority is that of *spiritual fitness*.

> For physical training is of some value (useful for a lit-
> tle), but godliness (spiritual training) is useful *and* of
> value in everything *and* in every way, for it holds prom-
> ise for the present life and also for the life which is to
> come (1 Tim. 4:8).

There is no cosmetic for the interior person. It is our union
with Christ that creates the inner beauty. The gentle and quiet
spirit is characteristic of the Spirit of Christ. If we were as concerned with the inner garments of the spirit as with our
wardrobes, if we looked upon the woman who models a beautiful
spirit and desired to look like her and were as concerned with spiritual fitness as with physical fitness, the Church would soon
become radiant in its worship and service to God.

THE BEAUTY OF FAITH

Let me introduce you to a beautiful woman I met in a book enti-
tled *His Part and Ours* by Sidlow Baxter. This remarkable story,
told by a Baptist minister, concerns a crippled woman living in
Australia who at age 18 contracted a disease which cost her the
loss of a foot. The disease progressed until she lost her other foot,
then her legs, hands, and arms, until nothing remained of her but
the trunk. It was in this condition that the minister found her.

> I found the walls of her room covered with texts, all of
> them speaking of joy and peace and power. . . .
> Hundreds of people had been converted or encouraged
> by the letters she had written. She lay in her bed and
> asked one day what she could do, a dismembered
> woman, without a joint in her body. Then an inspiration
> came to her, and she got a friend, who was a carpenter,
> to come, and he fitted a pad to her shoulder, and then to
> that . . . a pen, and she began to write letters with it. . . .
>
> She had received 1,500 letters from people who had
> been brought to Christ through the letters she had writ-
> ten from that room. When asked how she did it, she
> said, "Jesus said that they who believed on Him, out of
> them should flow rivers of living water. I believed on
> Him, and that is all."[3]

She believed on Him! What an example of a woman made
truly beautiful by the Spirit of Christ Who came to make His
home with her—a dismembered temple in which the Holy Spirit
was pleased to dwell. Her name is never mentioned, but I doubt
that I will ever forget her. She is another one I will seek out in
heaven. I want her to know how much she added to my journey.
Perhaps she will add something to yours.

It is one thing to read about such a woman, but to meet face-to-face with such a woman is something else again. I was introduced to Frieda through a newspaper article, and was so impacted by her story that I wanted others to know of her. The newspaper would not give me her whereabouts or her telephone number, so I had to rely on God to make it happen. About two years later, as I was having lunch at a favorite restaurant, I noticed a woman pushing a wheelchair toward me. Soon Frieda was seated at the table next to me.

"Excuse me, I don't want to intrude, but . . ." Frieda was delighted to know that someone would ask God to arrange a meeting with her, and just as pleased that He had. After eating lunch together we exchanged telephone numbers and made plans for a more lengthy visit in her home.

The most remarkable thing about Frieda is not that she has lived for 75 years without the benefit of arms and legs, but that there is no hint of defeat or self-pity about her. She spoke of the importance of her faith in God and the love she received from her mother. At one point in our conversation she raised her head as high as she could, locked her eyes onto mine, and said, "I always knew that I had a purpose!" I realized at that moment that Frieda was more whole than some of the women I could name.

Some would look at Frieda and say, what a cruel God to allow such a thing to happen. I look at Frieda and say, what an awesome God to sustain such a woman. When the old things have passed away and all things have been made new, when we are enjoying those things the Lord has prepared in Heaven for those who love Him, will Frieda, or others who have run the more difficult race, ever say they wish they had never been born?

Yes, Frieda, you have a purpose, one that reaches far beyond your 75 years. God works through you in ways you will never understand this side of heaven. Your life has spilled over into mine and I am richer for it, as are those I have spoken to about you. You give us all a great deal to think about!

SKIN-DEEP

Only the refiner of precious metals can vouch for the number of karats in a bar of gold. And only God can appraise the value of an individual. Any opinion apart from His will be faulty. This is true when we attempt to evaluate ourselves and others based on physical appearance. Our identity will never be stable if it depends on the response of others, because these "others" are subject to temperament swings and character traits that regulate their opinion of us.

Abraham Lincoln said, "The Lord prefers common-looking people. That is the reason He makes so many of them." Perhaps this was his way of coming to terms with his physical appearance. He was not considered a handsome man, but who can argue but that the beauty of his spirit left an indelible impression upon world history?

I knew a woman who recycled her birthday and Christmas gifts when they were not to her liking. She always put a great deal of effort into the wrapping, but the gift itself was always a disappointment. Some individuals come to us in spectacular wrappings but fail to live up to their packaging, whereas real beauty very often comes in plain wrappings. Physical beauty is to be used for the glory of God, not to build pedestals for ourselves. A woman who is all wrapped up in herself, no matter how beautiful she may appear on the surface, makes a very unattractive package.

> I appeal to you . . . in view of [all] the mercies of God, to make a decisive dedication of your bodies [presenting all your members and faculties] as a living sacrifice, holy (devoted, consecrated) and well pleasing to God, which is your reasonable (rational, intelligent) service *and* spiritual worship (Rom. 12:1).

Knowing this, we can ask God for a new perspective, praying that He give us the desire to become a woman dressed in the incorruptible beauty of the spirit. For it is His will that we be "conformed to the image of His dear Son," so that the "features" of our spirit resemble His (Rom. 8:29).

YOUR BODY?

If we consecrate our bodies to God, He will help us care for and use our bodies in a God-honoring manner. Until we do this, we cannot expect to overcome the excesses that directly affect our bodies, whether it be food, drugs, or alcohol. We cannot resist the aid of God and expect change to take place. We will never conquer our destructive eating habits in our own power. All eating disorders are a symptom of emotional pain. Many of our symptoms don't show. This one does! The first step to healthy eating habits and freedom from any substance abuse is to submit our body to God and invite Him into the source of the pain that lies behind the destructive behavior.

The same principle applies to the grief we so often experience with the aging process. We look in the mirror and wonder, *where is the woman I used to be?* This calls for a turning from what we used to be toward what we shall become. Our bodies are going to age, but our inner woman will grow more lovely year by year under the polishing of God's perfecting grace. May we resolve, with God's help, to model womanhood in a way that will honor God and inspire those who share our lives.

> But the godly shall flourish like palm trees, and grow tall as the cedars of Lebanon. For they are transplanted into the Lord's own garden, and are under His personal care. Even in old age they will still produce fruit and be vital and green (Ps. 92:12–14, TLB).

When Jesus spoke of the difficulty of the rich entering the Kingdom of Heaven, He was referring to the way in which the distractions of wealth can get in the way of making God first in our lives. And for the same distracting reasons, a preoccupation with beauty on the part of a woman has the potential to do the same. Like wealth, beauty can corrupt. Like wealth, beauty carries with it a particular responsibility. Whatever we have received, let us use it to the glory of God, not to call attention to ourselves.

There will always be women more attractive than you and me, as well as plenty of professionals who can remake our image, for a price. And what a price some have paid. God is sovereign over the womb (Ps. 119:13–15). He knew our days and our form before we were created. He has a plan for everybody, and for every *body*. His hands have made us (Job 10:8).

Eternal Beauty

If you have been seeking and knocking at the doors of the fashion and cosmetic houses for your identity, God invites you to ask, seek, and knock at the door of His Kingdom that you might obtain a more excellent beauty, one that even the grave cannot destroy. Submit the image you have of yourself to the One Who created you. You are much more than meets the eye! Get out of the competition and live as the "original" God made you to be.

We can dress for Christ, make ourselves attractive for Him, and do it with style, modesty, and the dignity befitting our union with Him. The woman who desires to be truly beautiful cannot sacrifice the adornment of her eternal spirit for the sake of her temporary body.

When we put the flesh under the light of Scripture, we acquire a greater respect for the body and are more inclined to think twice about how we present ourselves before the world. When you look in the mirror, remember that God also lives inside the body framed in the mirror.

No woman is more confident than the woman who has been groomed by the Holy Spirit. The world may not recognize her beauty, but the day is coming when she will stand before God and the hosts of Heaven, gloriously clothed in the robe of His righteousness.

Help us, gracious Lord, to respect our bodies as Your temple; to understand that nothing we do on the outside can take the place of what You can make of us on the inside; to overcome the habits that put our bodies at risk, and to present ourselves daily before the world in a manner worthy of our calling in Christ Jesus.

Notes

1. Andrew Murry, *The Spirit of Christ,* James Nesbit and Co., London, 1908, 236.
2. Joseph S. Exell, *The Bible Illustrator,* Baker Books, 1 Peter 3:3, 256.
3. Sidlow Baxter, *His Part and Ours* (Grand Rapids, Mich.: Zondervan Publishers, 1964), 33, 34.

9

Two Different Worlds

✠

The order in which we establish our priorities is always influenced by what is before us at the moment. We respond immediately to the cry of a child in distress, the smell of smoke in the house, and unfamiliar sounds in the middle of the night. But if in the steady stream of daily events we do not learn to separate what needs our attention now from what can wait, we are likely to become entangled in the less important at the expense of the more important. The same principle applies to our spiritual lives as well.

Up to this point we have focused upon the life of the woman. Now we expand that focus to examine the common ground shared by all who profess the Name of Christ. Here, in the shadow of the Cross, there is no longer male nor female, but a people who are called by His name. From now on our relationship with Christ takes precedence over all other relationships. Married or single, with or without children, no matter what our age, what most concerns us now is that *we live out our salvation in a manner worthy of our Savior.*

If you need an explanation as to why this priority is left to the latter chapters of the book, it is because it is most often in the latter chapters of our lives that we give it the priority it deserves. Our human relationships always claim the greater share of our attention, as do the demands of life itself. And without the help of the Holy Spirit, we will continue to lay aside spiritual priorities in favor of those of the natural world.

You and I are citizens of the country in which we live, and at the same time citizens of a Kingdom which is *not* of this world, and for as long as we live there will be a tug-of-war between the two. Here we run into the biggest hurdle of the Christian life. How do we operate in two different worlds simultaneously without losing our spiritual balance?

The Kingdom of God does not refer to a specific territory over which God is in control, but a condition within the life of the believer in which God is recognized as Sovereign over ALL things. Jesus, Who embodied the Kingdom said, "The Kingdom of God is within you [in your hearts] *and* among you [surrounding you]" (Luke 17:21).

The Kingdom signifies the new life of the believer, under the control of the Holy Spirit, through faith in Jesus Christ. It is the inner life of new perspectives concerning God, self, and eternity which shapes the character into "an irresistible force over which the gates of hell cannot prevail."[1]

> The Father has delivered *and* drawn us to Himself out of the control *and* the dominion of darkness and has transferred us into the Kingdom of the Son of His love (Col. 1:13).

When I transferred my citizenship from Canada to the United States, I was not required to change who I was as an individual. My attitudes and ambitions remained the same. I could live as easily in this country as I did in Canada just the way I was. The Kingdom of God operates differently. Once we are OF the Kingdom we must undergo some changes to make us fit for it. There is a Kingdom protocol to be learned, a Kingdom character to acquire, an attitude of worship and service to be developed.

For we are God's [own] handiwork (His workmanship), recreated in Christ Jesus, [born anew] that we may do those good works which God predestined (planned beforehand) for us [taking paths which He prepared ahead of time], that we should walk in them [living the good life which He prearranged and made ready for us to live] (Eph. 2:10).

American citizenship does not include easy access to the White House, but as citizens of the Kingdom, we are invited to present ourselves to our King at any time—day or night. He takes a personal interest in every detail concerning our lives and is eager to have us participate in His.

A HOLY ALLIANCE

We hear a great deal about the importance of having a personal relationship with Jesus Christ. But in the hearing of it do we really understand what it means? Or has the phrase been reduced to a sound bite in the explosion of information circulating within the church today?

The topic undertaken in this chapter calls for careful handling. To do this we must first understand the meaning of relationship. By today's standards the term can mean just about anything we want it to mean, as long as it fits our purpose. In order to *have* a personal relationship with Christ, we must accept His terms for such a relationship; otherwise, we are not speaking the same language. God always intended that we live in relationship with Him as a Person, not as an idea, a force, or a philosophy. But He chose another word to describe it, and that word is *covenant.*

Know, recognize, *and* understand therefore that the Lord your God, He is God, the faithful God, Who keeps covenant and steadfast love *and* mercy with those who love Him and keep His commandments, to a thousand generations (Deut. 7:9).

A covenant is a formal agreement or treaty between two parties with each assuming some obligation. A covenant may also be imposed by a greater power upon a lesser one, whereby the greater power demands loyalty and obligates itself to the welfare of the lesser one.

To put this into perspective for us today, we have entered into a covenant of salvation, initiated by God through Christ, in which He commits (promises) Himself to our eternal welfare—and requires our loyalty in return. When we speak of the importance of a personal relationship with Christ, we are stressing the importance of *committing (promising) ourselves to Christ.*

BEFORE AND AFTER

Prior to the coming of Christ men learned about God through human teachers. Now God the Son was doing the teaching. It was the King of kings explaining the Kingdom to those who would ultimately inherit it. He not only teaches, but lives out His teaching all the way to the Cross.

How can we understand the love of a Savior Who gave Himself for us before we even came into existence? How do we translate His sacred sufferings on our behalf into human terms? His was an agony that exceeded the limits of physical pain to endure the spiritual torture of bearing the sins of all humanity, and what must have been the agonies of agonies, to know beforehand that there would be those who would come to gawk, to ridicule, and to trample the love of God. Yet He counted His sufferings as secondary to our salvation and the will of the Father before the cost.

We can only marvel at why God chose to make Himself

vulnerable to the fickle human heart. In spite of our broken promises and flirtatious advances in time of need—even when we keep changing the locks to the doors of our hearts—His love endures. It is not by accident that God expresses His love for humanity in terms of the marriage covenant, or that He reveals Himself as the Husband of His people.

> For your Maker is your husband—the Lord of hosts is His Name—and the Holy One of Israel is your Redeemer: the God of the whole earth He is called (Isa. 54:5).

> And I will betroth you to Me forever; yes I will betroth you to Me in righteousness and justice, in steadfast love and in mercy. I will even betroth you to Me in stability *and* in faithfulness, and you shall know (recognize, be aquainted with, appreciate, give heed to, and cherish) the Lord (Hos. 2:19–20).

God is teaching us about commitment—to Himself, and to each other—and He further verifies the sanctity of marriage and the family in describing Himself as the Bridegroom and His church as His beloved Bride (Matt. 22:1–14; Matt. 25:1–13; John 3:29, 30).

In the exchange of wedding vows a man and a woman pledge to be faithful to one another in a covenant of marriage, and in so doing each puts aside all former loyalties for the good of the marriage. We say "I do" to God when we receive Jesus as Savior and Lord of our lives. We are now identified by His Name and pledged to bear the fruit that reflects our covenant union with Him. The Sovereign of the universe has made us His own. He is our God and we are His people. Unfortunately, this sacred agreement is often taken lightly after the first glow of salvation has been realized.

One day, as I sought a deeper understanding of what it means to live in covenant with Christ, I was overcome with the desire to recite my covenant vows.

> *I, Donna, take you, Jesus, for my Lord and Savior, to love and to cherish from this day forward, for better or for worse, in sickness and in health, for richer or for poorer, not just in this life, Lord, but forever.*

The words were no more out of my mouth before I was struck with the realization that my Lord had already taken me at Calvary. For better or for worse, in sickness of body or soul, in spiritual poverty or material need, the pledge of God in Christ had always been mine—held in trust throughout the ages until the day of my discovery.

> The joy we experience in knowing that we belong to Christ and He belongs to us is second only to His joy in imparting this understanding to us, for we now become the fruit of the travail of His soul (Isa. 53:11). His joy is in those who reverence Him. His pleasure is in His people (Ps. 149:4; Ps. 147:11).
>
> And He died for all, so that all those who live might live no longer to and for themselves, *but to and for Him* Who died and was raised again for their sake (2 Cor. 5:15). (Emphasis added)

IN HIS MAJESTY'S SERVICE

As God purposed the union between man and woman in marriage to populate the earth, our covenant union with Christ is intended to populate Heaven. We who have been delivered from the kingdom of darkness are obligated to God on behalf of those yet to be delivered, for the One Who gave Himself for us desires that "all come to the knowledge of the truth" (1 Tim. 2:4).

Everything that benefits the Kingdom benefits those who inherit the Kingdom. As co-heirs with Christ we become *co-laborers* with Christ, and we serve with the understanding that service rendered is immediately credited to the good of the servant.

> Vast fields of human souls are ripening all around us and are ready now for reaping. The reapers will be paid good wages and will be gathering eternal souls into the granaries of heaven! What joys await the sower and the reaper, both together (John 4:35,36, TLB).

As an employer matches dollar for dollar what his employees put away for retirement, we have spiritual treasure laid up for us in Heaven. This is not a case of trying to bribe God for eternal favors, but of responding to the will of God. We serve not out of a desire for rewards, but out of love for our Lord and Master. The reward system is His plan, not ours. It is not self-serving, but God-serving (Matt. 25:14–23; Luke 16:1–13; Eph. 6:8).

Each of us is given a particular field in which to labor. Within this field lies a potential harvest of the good works God has prepared for us through our talents, resources, family history, circumstances, and the number of years allotted to us. What determines the harvest is our willingness to cultivate the particular ground chosen for us according to the will of God and the degree to which we respond to Him according to His revealed Word. I became a committed Christian the day my Savior spoke to me from His Word, saying:

> Anyone who is not for Me is against Me; if he isn't helping Me, he is hurting My cause (Luke 11:23, TLB). The Amplified version says, He who is not with Me (siding

and believing with Me) is against Me, and he who does not gather with Me [engage in My interest], scatters.

There are many passages in the Bible which are difficult to understand, but *this is not one of them!* The only way to dodge this passage is to turn our backs on it, and to do this we also turn our backs on the One speaking the message. And we do well to consider again just exactly Who is speaking.

> The exact likeness of the unseen God . . . the Creator Who made everything in heaven and earth, the things we can see and the things we can't; the spirit world with its kings and kingdoms, its rulers and authorities; all were made by Christ for His Own use and glory. He was before all else began and it is His power that holds everything together (Col. 1:15,16,17, TLB selected).

A MATTER OF ATTITUDE

An elderly man was having difficulty navigating the steps on his way out of church one Sunday morning. His daughter (visibly annoyed and doing her best to hurry him out of the building) said, "I don't know why you persist in coming to church when it takes so much out of you!" He turned toward me and said, "She doesn't understand how important it is to me just to be able to show which side I'm on." What a witness this man has been to me. Someday I'll search him out in Heaven and tell him how much he has contributed to my journey. And I pray that there is never any question as to which side *I'm* on!

What a contrast between this man's attitude and the woman who didn't want to know the Holy Spirit because she might have to change. In her determination to quench the influence of the Spirit in her life, she was actually siding with the spiritual forces that operate against God. The same could be said of the young woman who didn't like the Living Bible translation because it was too easy to understand.

> For whatever God says to us is full of living power: it is sharper than the sharpest dagger, cutting swift and deep into our innermost thoughts and desires with all their parts, exposing us for what we really are. Everything about us is bare and wide open to the all-seeing eyes of our living God; nothing can be hidden from Him to Whom we must explain all that we have done (Heb. 4:12–13, TLB, selected).

Our human nature is offended by these reminders. Something rises up on the inside of us and complains, "Lighten up! After all, I'm only human!" And that is precisely the point! This is why God invaded the human condition in the Person of Jesus Christ.

Mark Twain spoke for many of us when he said, "It isn't what I don't understand in the Bible that bothers me, but what I do understand." It is the "bothering" of the Holy Spirit that reveals our spiritual poverty and desperate need of God. This is how God courts the soul and moves it to cry out, "Create in me a clean heart, O God; and renew a right spirit within me" (Ps. 51:10).

A CHANGE OF HEART

Much is written and preached about our failing—because we do fail. And as much is said about the grace of God available to us when we mess up. So how do we reconcile the inconsistencies of the flesh with the high calling of Jesus Christ that requires us to consummate our love for Him through obedience?

If you [really] love Me you will keep (obey) My commands (John 14:15). Why do you call me, Lord, Lord and do not [practice] what I tell you (Luke 6:46)?

If we will acknowledge His right to our lives, He will prepare us to do all that He requires of us. It is the power of the Holy Spirit which facilitates obedience and makes it more and more uncomfortable to live the way we used to live, but we must first *choose* obedience before we can *practice* obedience. God will never override our free will, but once the heart is opened He comes in to work in us a change of heart.

Obedience signifies attentive hearing with compliant submission and agreement and is:

- a demonstration of our love for Christ (Luke 6:46).
- the will of God demonstrated by the life of Christ (Luke 11:28; James 1:22).
- a spiritual discipline initiated and enabled by the Holy Spirit (1 Peter 1:2).
- what produces the acceptable fruit of our lives (James 1:22).
- what identifies us as true followers of Christ (John 15:8).
- the power behind our prayers (John 15:7).
- the best protection against the forces of evil (James 4:7; Eph. 6:13–18).
- our highest praise and worship (Matt. 15:8, 9).

A LEARNING PROCESS

I live with an Australian shepherd named Hannah, a sweet-natured dog who is usually anxious to please. But something comes over Hannah when we start playing ball. At first she returns the ball and drops it into my hand so I can throw it again. But as the game progresses, she becomes more possessive of the ball and less willing to give it up. When this happens, I call a halt to the game. Hannah hasn't figured out how the game works. I don't think she is deliberately trying to be obstinate; she is just acting true to her dog nature.

God will often call a halt to our activities for our own good. Sometimes His intervention is painful. We forget that while His love is unconditional, His promises are not! This is where we must separate the truth from wishful thinking. The consequences of having our own way is that we will *suffer the consequences* of having our own way, and in all probability, so will those who love us.

Hannah is a little over a year old; she still has much to learn. Only time will tell if she is going to change the way she plays ball with me, and only eternity will show how willing we were to give God what He desired of us. When we fail to respond to Him, we show our lack of concern for His feelings. Yes, God has feelings! He feels grief, anger, and rejection. In Genesis 6:6 we find this sorrowful confession: "The Lord was grieved that he had made man on the earth, and his heart was filled with pain."

We have been sealed (marked, branded) as God's own possession. How then can we neglect so Holy a union? Should it not be tended with reverence? With feeling?

> Don't cause the Holy Spirit sorrow by the way you live. Remember, He is the One who marks you to be present on that day when salvation from sin will be complete (Eph. 4:30, TLB).

William Huntington said that one of the sharpest sensations of pain he ever felt was after he was quickened by divine grace and overcome with pity for God. I had a similar reaction during a struggle with forgiveness. It was sympathy for God that prompted me to forgive what up until then I saw as unforgivable. When I considered the toll on His heart over the millions of deceived, rebellious, and wounded of the world, my heart broke for Him.

What dissolves the outrage over the inequities of life, and the debates surrounding them, is the blinding awareness of the heart of God in all of this. In spite of the pain we heap upon Him—He pities His children. In spite of our arguments against Him—He remembers that we are dust.

Once the long suffering of God is allowed to penetrate the suffering of self, we grieve with Him and want to do nothing to further bruise His heart. From now on for us to live is Christ! No longer dispassionate concerning the plan of God, we enlist in the service of the King of kings to partner with Him in the will of the Father. It is an awareness of the suffering of God that insists we grow up and get on with our Father's business!

We were supposed to manage the earth. When we failed, God didn't boot the human race out of office, but gave Himself as a remedy for our failures. Because we could not walk in His shoes, God walked in our shoes and left a clear trail for us to follow. There are a number of reasons—all of them human—why we misread, mistrust, or ignore the road signs. Some are the result of ignorance. Most can be classified as SIN.

Jesus said, "My food (nourishment) is to do the will (pleasure) of Him Who sent Me and to accomplish and completely finish His work" (John 4:34). If this is what sustained the life of Christ, how can we expect to live out our salvation in a manner worthy of Him by any other means?

No Neutral Ground

We will never come to faith in Christ without first responding to the conviction of the Holy Spirit. And we will not lay aside the self for the sake of God if we do not continue to respond, *on a daily basis,* to the ongoing mentoring of the Spirit. We want what the Kingdom has to offer, not always what the Kingdom *requires.* We run to where signs and wonders are evident, but drag our feet when asked to embrace the Cross and the death of our self-interests for the interests of the Kingdom.

The lukewarm and Cross-avoiding Christian does not further the Kingdom and will most certainly play into the hands of Satan and his agenda. If he can't stop us from believing in Christ, he will attempt to make us *unfruitful* for Christ. And one of his most effective weapons is to make us think he doesn't exist.

I was shocked to hear a woman who had attended a church for more than 30 years say that Satan was just a metaphor for evil. Nothing could change her mind, not even the Word of God as taught by her own pastor. She wanted no part of it and would *have* no part of it. She chose to remain a disciple of her own opinions, and in so doing she became a pawn in a strategy that flourishes when those who are about to come under attack have no sense of danger.

We find a tragic illustration of what happens when people refuse to see things for what they really are in the history of World War II. The moment the Swiss government voted to live out the war as a neutral nation, they began working for the enemy. Neutrality is always in the eye of the one professing it. It is also short-lived, and it will quickly land us on one side of the fence or the other, to the benefit of one party or another. As surely as history proved there was no neutral ground during Hitler's rampage, the judgment seat of Christ will prove there is no neutral ground in the universal conflict between God and Satanic forces.

You and I will answer for our involvement or lack of involvement in the cause of Christ. We cannot vote ourselves out of the war. Let us not be seduced into thinking that we can stay out of it, live and let live, and be none the worse for it, or think that the enemy will leave us alone—he won't. He'll use us to his advantage to undermine our relationships with God and each other, and even go so far as to employ us to do his work for him! If we are not involved in Kingdom activities, we are aiding the enemy.

Everything Jesus did was backed by divine intention. He was about his Father's business! And like the first band of disciples who made up the early church, He is sending us today.

> Jesus said to His disciples: We must work the works of Him Who sent Me *and* be busy with His business while it is daylight; night is coming on, when no man can work (John 9:4).

> Then Jesus said to them again, Peace to you! [Just] as the Father has sent Me forth, so I am sending you. And having said this, He breathed on them and said to them, Receive the Holy Spirit! (John 20:21–22).

If we are to continue the works of Christ, we must stay close to the Power Source. If we are to live out our salvation in a manner worthy of Him, we must remain committed to the One Who has received us into His Kingdom.

END TIMES?

In the midst of all the speculation in the church today concerning the end times and our Lord's return, we cannot forget the 145,000 souls throughout the world who come to an end of *their* times every 24 hours.[2] Each time you and I take a breath, some one else runs out of breath.

As beneficiaries of the new covenant in Christ we are called to a life of stewardship over our time, talents, and resources, for the sake of the 145,000. *For their night is coming; their time of hearing and decision will be no more!* Out of reverence and gratitude for all our Savior has done for us, let us devote our lives to the will of the Father as He did. Only when we live out the Gospel do we fulfill our destiny as He intended (Matt. 5:13–16).

God is looking for committed hearts through which He can minister to the needs of humanity. He hears the cry of the lost and needy of the world and passes that cry onto His covenant people.

How many times, Lord, have You reminded me to do unto others as I would have them do unto me? Now You turn a familiar coin to reveal another side and say, "Do to others as you would have Me do unto *you!*" The self-serving me is paying more attention to this side of the coin.

You said if I offer food and drink to one in need I offer it to You. If I comfort the sick, I comfort You. I ask You to bless and save my children. You ask me to remember the orphan, and remind me that I was once one of the least of these. I ask for your provision and protection daily. You ask me to share with those who cannot provide for themselves.

You ask only for what You have given. How can I deny a love that urges me to lay up for myself a treasure in a Kingdom prepared for me from the foundation of the world? (see Matt. 25:34)

As the strength of a chain is measured by its weakest link, so the depth of our love for Christ will show in our response to those He has chosen to identify Himself with. We are not to judge the reason for their circumstances, but regard them for what they are—the "least of these" spoken of in one of the most chilling passages in the Word of God—for in our compassion toward the least of these is our faithfulness to Christ reflected (Matt. 25:35–46).

> For we must all appear *and* be revealed as we are before the judgment seat of Christ, so that each one may receive [his pay] according to what he has done in the body, whether good or evil [considering what his purpose and motive have been, and what he has achieved, been busy with, and given himself and his attention to accomplishing] (2 Cor. 5:10).

God never contradicts Himself, therefore we must always emphasize that our Christian *works do not save us,* but are the *evidence* of our salvation through our faith in the finished work of Christ. We cannot work and earn our way *into* Heaven, but we are to do good works on our way *to* Heaven.

> Let your light so shine before men that they may see your moral excellence *and* your praiseworthy, noble and good deeds and recognize *and* honor *and* praise *and* glorify your Father Who is in heaven (Matt. 5:16).

This light, these noble, good, and God-honoring deeds, are the fruits of our faith—the outcome of a *wholehearted* response to the covenant proposal of everlasting love and life through Christ—and the faithfulness of our covenant keeping God.

ALL IN THE FAMILY

Those who have been mentored by the Holy Spirit for any length of time are to glorify God by their attitudes toward the less mature, demonstrating the same love and patience with which God has endured with them. Living in covenant with God includes living in covenant with one another. We are to encourage our siblings in the faith, remembering where we were when we were delivered from the kingdom of darkness. It is wisdom to pray against the temptation of pride and attitudes of competition and judgment toward our covenant brothers and sisters.

> And let us consider *and* give attentive, continuous care to watching over one another, studying how we may stir up (stimulate and incite) to love and helpful deeds *and* noble activities (Heb. 10:24).

> For we are fellow workmen (joint promoters, laborers together) with *and* for God; *you* are God's garden *and* vineyard and field under cultivation, [you are] God's building (1 Cor. 3:9).

These are the people we are going to spend eternity with! So let's get to know and love each other now. Authentic love is an attraction to others. The world is watching. Are we different? Have we anything to offer the lost, the hurting, the needy? *We must not overlook the importance of the love "light" we reflect one to another in the furthering of the Kingdom.*

> This is My commandment: that you love one another [just] as I have loved you (John 15:12). By this shall all [men] know that you are My disciples, if you love one another [if you keep on showing love among yourselves] (John 13:35).

The Holy Spirit is given that we might serve God and each other. But we must remember that we are gifted for His purposes and not our own. We can do many good things but for the wrong reasons. And there is a very fine line between relating what wonderful things God is doing without calling attention to the fact that He is doing them through us.

> But let him who glories, glory in this: that he understands and knows Me [personally and practically, directly discerning and recognizing My character], that I am the Lord, Who practices loving-kindness, judgment, and righteousness in the earth, for in these things I delight, says the Lord (Jer. 9:24; 1 Cor. 1:31; 2 Cor. 10:17).

For the joy that was set before Him, our Lord endured the Cross. We are that joy: His beloved, His inheritance, His people. And now, for the joy that is set before us as His covenant people, let us press on to lay hold of that for which He has laid hold of us and made us His own, until our lives become an ongoing act of worship.

The cost of our priorities is never realized until they have actually cost us something, and with this in mind, it's time to take into account the priority of prayer in the operation of the Kingdom and the part we are to play in this holy exercise.

Notes

1.   Joseph S. Exell, *The Bible Illustrator,* Luke, Vol. 3, Ch. 17, Baker Books, 310.
2.   *Universal Almanac of World Statistics,* 1996.

10

IF GOD IS SOVEREIGN
WHY PRAY?

✝

Considering that our union with Christ is also a school for Heaven, if we are to complete the curriculum we must learn to pray. And to pray effectively we pray in the same way Jesus taught His disciples to pray: in faith, persistence, humility, repentance, with a spirit of forgiveness toward those who have wronged us. And to do it all *in His name.*

We must ask and keep on asking, with the faith of a child running to meet a beloved Father, expecting to be welcomed and responded to. The reason we *can* expect to have our prayers answered is that we do pray in the name of Jesus. But this is far more than the tacking of three words onto the end of a prayer. Our prayers take on a new purpose once we understand that to pray in the name of Jesus is *to pray in His character and in harmony with His will.*

The topic of prayer plunges us into a mystery every bit as puzzling as the Trinity. While we cannot know all there is to know concerning this mystery either, our Lord made it clear that we are to participate IN the mystery. Nothing contributes more to the fruit-bearing process in the life of the believer than prayer, for it is in prayer that we gain access to the power of God. And we are to use it for the same purpose for which Christ came into the world:

to satisfy the will of the Father.

We pray because Jesus prayed, and because, as John Guest explains, "We are spiritual beings, who live and move and have our being in the realm of spirit. Hence prayer is critical as the underpinning of our whole life, not just for its usefulness in solving our problems. The key to living fully and freely in the kingdom of God is prayer."[1]

When we pray in the name of Jesus, we team up with God to cause to be what He wills to be. Amazing! But there is much more going on here than what we are aware of. Prayer sets off a chain of events in the life of the person who prays as well as the one prayed for. It is as if God turns the tables on us by applying our prayers to the work of Romans 8:29. In the words of Richard Foster:

> To pray is to change. Prayer is the central avenue God uses to transform us. If we are unwilling to change, we will abandon prayer as a noticeable characteristic of our lives. The closer we come to the heartbeat of God the more we see our need and the more we desire to be conformed to Christ. . . . All who have walked with God have viewed prayer as the main business of their lives.[2]

THY WILL BE DONE

Herbert Lockyer, author of *All the Doctrines of the Bible,* writes, "Prayer is both a privilege and a necessity, for without its exercise we are cut off from the Source of life, light and love. . . . Christ constantly urged his followers to make it the chief business of their lives to pray. From His own example we learn the necessity of prayer. . . . One of the greatest of all prayer secrets is to pray in the realm of Bible truth and language."[3] And in Andrew Murray's classic book, *With Christ in the School of Prayer,* we are introduced to the divine order of this holy practice:

> While we ordinarily first bring our own needs to God in prayer, and then think of what belongs to God and his interests, the Master reverses the order. First, *Thy* name, *Thy* kingdom, *Thy* will; then, give us, forgive us, lead us, deliver us. The lesson is of more importance than we think. The sooner I learn to forget myself in the desire that He may be glorified, the richer will the blessing be that prayer will bring to myself. No one ever loses by what he sacrifices for the Father.
>
> This must influence all our prayer. There are two sorts of prayer: personal and intercessory. The latter ordinarily occupies the lesser part of our time and energy. This may not be. Christ has opened the school of prayer specially to train intercessors for the great work of bringing down, by their faith and prayer, the blessings of His work and love on the world around. There can be no deep growth in prayer unless this be made our aim . . . Jesus would train us to the blessed life of consecration and service, in which our interests are all subordinate to the Name, and the Kingdom, and the Will of the Father.[4]

God welcomes our prayers when we are young in the same way a mother is delighted with a picture colored by her child, even though the colors may not be confined within the lines. Once the child advances to grade school and is capable of more, she expects to see the coloring improve, and it will, because coloring is a favorite pastime for children; they get a lot of practice. It is the same with prayer.

In its beginning prayer is so simple that the feeble child can pray, yet it is at the same time the highest and holiest work to which man can rise. It is fellowship with the Unseen and Most Holy One. The powers of the eternal world have been placed at its disposal. It is . . . the channel of all blessings, the secret of power and life. Not only for ourselves, but for others, for the Church, for the world, it is to prayer that God has given the right to take hold of Him and His strength. It is on prayer that the promises wait for their fulfillment, the kingdom for its coming, the glory of God for its full revelation. All of this must be learned. It can only be learned in the school of much prayer, for practice makes perfect. The deep undertone of all our prayer must be the teachableness that comes from a sense of ignorance, and from faith in Christ as the perfect teacher. Only then will we learn to pray in power.[5]

If we are indifferent to prayer, we are living beneath our privilege and calling and robbing God of our service. In her book *Intercession,* Joy Dawson delivers an important challenge to those of us who call ourselves Christians.

Every believer has the privilege of being used by God in effective intercession. *Not* just the favored few. *Not* just little old ladies who are not able to do much else. *Not* just people who are "specially called to the ministry of intercession," as I so often hear. Intercession is *everyone's* ministry, just as worshipping and witnessing are. The Bible does not even suggest that to become an intercessor one must be specially gifted. Jesus Christ . . . alone is our role model. And He modeled prayer as a daily priority for everyone.[6]

ON EARTH

When we pray for the redemption of the lost, for physical or emotional healing, for the mending of relationships, or for material needs, we know that God alone holds the blueprint for the lives of those we pray for. We also know that He desires to give that which will complement His plans for them, and in aligning our prayers with His will, we trigger the greatest power in the universe.

> If you live in Me [abide vitally united to Me] and My words remain in you *and* continue to live in your hearts, ask whatever you will, and it shall be done for you (John 15:7).

> And this is the confidence (the assurance, the privilege of boldness) which we have in Him: [we are sure] that if we ask anything (make any request) according to His will (in agreement with His Own plan) He listens to *and* hears us. And if (since) we [positively] know that He listens to us in whatever we ask, we also know [with settled and absolute knowledge] that we have [granted us as our present possessions] the requests made of Him (1 John 5:14–15).

Prayer offered in the name of Jesus, according to His revealed nature and purpose, has the full weight of His authority behind it because we have asked for those things in keeping with the character of God.

As It Is in Heaven

We may only be able to hazard a guess at the inner workings of God's plan," [writes Douglas Kelly] "but we can know that as we pray, *Thy will be done* on the basis of His written Word, our prayers are being caught in the eternal purposes of God. There, in the grinding of the wheels of providence, they are somehow being used to activate the eternal decrees of God. . . . That is why tremendous things occur when believers pray *Your will be done.* The secret is to take God's promises and desires as expressed in Scripture and make them the basis of intercession.[7]

The condition for true prayer is abiding in Christ through our daily feeding upon the Scriptures. When we follow what Jesus taught concerning prayer, the end result will be answered prayer. Fixing God's word in our hearts and minds will change the very character of our prayers to conform them to the character and will of Christ.

We've already seen the importance of prayer in family relationships, but our Lord wants us prayerfully involved on a much grander scale. Whatever concerns our Lord *must* be of concern to His people. Without a sincere concern for others we cannot enter into the effectual fervent prayer that is "dynamic in its working." (James 5:16).

Me and Mine and His

Anyone who has experienced a slipped disc knows what an excruciating and debilitating condition it is. Many mature Christians were praying for me, and I knew that even out of this some good would come, although I questioned God more than once during the ordeal. I wanted to be free of pain and off and running, but

God would use the instrument of pain to make a much-needed adjustment in my prayer life.

I was praying for the strength to make it through another night when I began to weep, not for myself, but because I was suddenly confronted with how much of my prayer time was focused on my pain, with no thought of those who suffered as much if not more than I—particularly those in third-world countries without the benefit of pain medication.

The message I was getting was: If you love Me, pray for those who are afflicted with the same condition you suffer from. Pray for those who suffer alone with no one to pray for them. My mind was flooded with every imaginable form of suffering. It was as if God had opened a window to the world to show me the sufferings *of* the world. I prayed for those with back conditions, the forgotten in nursing homes, those destined to step into eternity before morning, for victims of abuse and of war—and I grew smaller and smaller in my own eyes.

As I continued to appeal to God on behalf of others, my own condition improved. I'm not trying to make a method out of my experience—I only know that in the midst of my pain I learned to pray as much for the concerns of His heart as I do for those of my own.

I shared this with a friend whose daughter is in a cult. She now prays not only for her daughter, but for those who introduced her to the cult, all who belong to the cult, and the parents who share her pain of having a child say, "Your God will not be my God." Another friend is battling cancer. She prays for every patient who frequents the cancer treatment center with her, and she sees this as her most important service to God. I cannot credit myself with the change in my attitude toward prayer. It was the transforming work of the Holy Spirit.

THE SWEETEST FRUIT

There is another group of people in dire need of prayer, and those directed to pray for these needy ones would seem the least likely to be chosen for the task.

> Invoke blessings upon *and* pray for the happiness of those who curse you, implore God's blessing (favor) upon those who abuse you [who revile, reproach, disparage, and high-handedly misuse you] (Luke 6:28).

We often forget that it was not only for our sins that Jesus died, but for the sins perpetrated upon us by others. If He was willing to pay the penalty for those offenses, is it so much for us to pray for them for the sake of God? Within the grand scheme of things there is a spiritual economy, and in this instance prayerful obedience will purchase two things: medication for our wounds, and the privilege of participating in the working of God's will in the life of the one who has harmed us.

After praying ten years for a woman I will call Rita, I was finally reunited with her. All I wanted was an opportunity to tell her what I'd received from God and see her share in those same blessings. Where she spent eternity was far more important than the grief she had caused me years earlier. During our three days together I made no mention of the past but spoke only of Jesus.

As I thought about it later, I could imagine how God had planned it: how from the time I came to live with her as a girl of 15, continuing through the difficult years that passed between us, God was preparing *me* to testify of Him as surely as He was preparing *her* to receive Him. And somewhere in Heaven it must have been recorded that on this very day, Rita would be touched by the same redemptive power that I'd experienced.

When I was a girl I wanted to become a part of her family, but now, with Rita approaching 80, God had put us together in *His* family. And although I was not aware of it at the time, her husband had been paying careful attention from another room in the house. Two years later he became a Christian.

In the commandment to pray for those who have injured us, God holds out the seed for the sweetest fruit of our lives, for in praying for these we show that we are true children of our Father in Heaven (Matt. 5:44–45). How many lives have been changed because someone said "yes" to God, and prayed for those most difficult to pray for? How many more are yet to be prayed for? How many souls are yet to be harvested? By giving us this specific prayer assignment, God is also assuring us that He intends to respond to our prayers.

A piece of paper was found lying near the body of a dead child in the Ravensbruck Nazi concentration camp where 98,000 men, women, and children were murdered. On the paper was written this prayer:

> O Lord, remember not only the men and women of good will, but also those of ill will. But do not only remember the suffering they have inflicted on us; remember the fruits we bought, thanks to this suffering: our comradeship, our loyalty, our humility, the courage, the generosity, the greatness of heart which has grown out of all this. And when they come to judgment, let all the fruits that we have borne be their forgiveness.[8]

If this tortured soul could offer such a prayer, how can we ignore the One Who commands us to pray for those who have wronged us? How can we deny Him the pleasure of our prayers? Why deny ourselves the privilege of serving Him this way?

God desires our prayers not only for those who add to our lives, but for those who subtract from our lives. And by giving God what He desires of us, we demonstrate our love and appreciation for

Him. The only way to deal with adversity is to recognize it as an opportunity for prayer—learning what Jesus taught by *living out* what He taught. It was in the midst of completing this chapter that I ran into a situation (during a routine trip to the grocery store) which further illustrates this truth.

I was holding the grocery cart with one hand and opening the trunk of my car with the other when I felt the cart move. Then I noticed a passing car and a boy trying to get into the front seat. My immediate reaction was, *How could that woman take off before her child is safely in the car?* But that was not the case at all. The boy (who could not have been more than ten years old) had my purse and was scrambling back into the car with it! My concern for the boy's safety was now concern for his future. I was already praying for him as I ran to call the police. This upsetting incident turned for good the moment I began to pray. While the boy and the woman had gained access to my property, *I had gained access into their lives through prayer.*

Satan has targeted this child for evil. I will target this child for good, as will those who have already joined me in this prayer assignment. It is only the privilege of serving God through intercession for these individuals which removes the sting of having to replace what was stolen. How appropriate to this situation are the words of John Stott concerning intercession: "Somehow it enables us to enter the field of spiritual conflict, and to align ourselves with the good purposes of God, so that his power is released and the principalities of evil are bound."[9] May it be so in the life of this one child, dear Lord, and for the one who is training him to serve Satan and not You.

Whenever this incident crosses my mind I take it as a reminder to pray for those involved. The loss of material possessions can not compare to the eternal destiny of a child.

The Night He Prayed for You and Me

We find the "Holy of Holies" of prayer recorded in the 17th chapter of John. The only way to approach this prayer is with hearts bowed, for we are about to eavesdrop as the Savior empties His heart before His Father. Consider carefully how this prayer is proportioned: verses 1–8 for Himself, and the remainder of the prayer (verses 9–26) for His disciples and those who would believe in Him from that time on.

As He prepares for the agony of the Cross, consider how He remembers you and me. Take it one step further and consider that He prayed for you. Consider also how, just before His most dreaded hours, He made provision for your most dreaded hours; how in laying down His will for the will of the Father He paved your way to the very gates of Heaven.

I ask you right now to lay this book aside, pick up your Bible, turn to John 17 and read this prayer, asking the Holy Spirit to teach you. If you are familiar with it, read it again, asking for a fresh vision for all it contains. Remember that He continues to intercede for us in agreement with the will of the Father and the Holy Spirit. This is the prayer of agreement over which no demonic power can prevail: God releasing the remedy for which we are pleading to the benefit of individuals and circumstances in accordance with His established Word and purpose.

A Good Investment

It is an act of gratitude toward the mercy of God to earnestly pray for those who have yet to discover His mercy. And in praying for our children and grandchildren, let us not forget the children without praying parents. God would have us always to pray for "the least of these." The next time you walk out of your house, remember those who live behind bars. He died for the least of these and the worst of these, and there but for His grace go you and I.

If your marriage runs into difficulty, pray for marriages in similar distress. Unemployed? Pray for those who share your concerns. Are you fighting cancer or some other life-threatening disease? Pray for those engaged in the same struggle. Whatever your need, allot a portion of your prayer time for those with similar needs. In praying for others you minister to them, to your own condition, and to our Lord. As Christians we are to live in such a way that others will know that God has not forgotten them. There is no better expression of this than to bring their names and concerns to Him in prayer.

We can invest the time we would otherwise waste in line at the checkout counter, stalled in traffic, or waiting in a doctor's office. It takes only a few seconds to pray: "Lord, I lift up every person in this place and ask that Your redemptive will be done in their lives that none be lost. And may those who already know You come to know You better and commit more fully to Your plan for their lives." We turn an ordinary day into an extraordinary day when we take advantage of these brief prayerful moments, and any prayer based on redemption is going to impact eternity.

> "The life of the Son of God in the believer," writes Oswald Chambers, "is nourished not by food but by prayer. When we pray on the basis of redemption, God creates something He can create no other way than through intercessory prayer. As a saved soul, the real business of your life is intercessory prayer. Whatever circumstances God may place you in, always pray immediately that His atonement may be as fully understood in the lives of others as it has been in yours. Pray for your friends *now,* and pray for those with whom you come in contact *now.*"[10]

Every believer can access the power of God for a world that is always in need of prayer. In Matt. 9:38 Jesus tells us to "pray the Lord of the harvest to send laborers into His harvest." If you continue to pray this way, God may send you out, or He may permit you to equip somebody else so they can go. But to pray this way is to participate in the gathering of the harvest even if you are not actually going into the mission field. Jesus made it clear that the labor supply is dependent upon prayer. Pray! Let prayer become the very rhythm of your life!

The Apostle Paul prayed that the Colossians would lead a life worthy of the Lord, "bearing fruit in every good work and increasing in the knowledge of God" (Col. 1:10). Our Lord said, "When you bear (produce) much fruit, My Father is honored *and* glorified, and you show *and* prove yourselves to be true followers of Mine" (John 15:8). The dedicated life bears the fruit of dedication; it seeks not its own end, but that which is profitable to God.

> I am the True Vine and My Father is the Vinedresser. Any branch in Me that does not bear fruit [that stops bearing] He cuts away (trims off, takes away); He cleanses *and* repeatedly prunes every branch that continues to bear fruit, to make it bear more *and* richer *and* more excellent fruit. I am the Vine; you are the branches. Whoever lives in Me and I in him bears much (abundant) fruit. However, apart from Me [cut off from vital union with Me] you can do nothing (John 15:1, 2, 5).

Let us pray for one another that *together,* as living members in the Body of Christ, our lives will be worthy of our Lord—that *together,* we bear fruit in every good work and increase in the knowledge of Him—that *together* we glorify the Father by showing ourselves to be disciples, true followers, of Christ.

Lord, teach us to pray.

Notes

1. John Guest, *Only a Prayer Away* (Ann Arbor, Mich.: Servant Publications/ Vine Books, 1985), 36.

2. Richard J. Foster, *Celebration of Discipline* (New York: HarperCollins Publishers, 1996), 30.

3. Herbert Lockyer, *All the Doctrines of the Bible* (Grand Rapids, Mich.: Zondervan Publishing, 1964), 225, 228.

4. Andrew Murray, *In the School of Prayer with Christ* (New York: M. A. Donohue Publishers), 36.

5. Ibid., 14.

6. Joy Dawson, *Intercession* (Seattle: Ywam Publishing, 1997), 22, 23.

7. Douglas F. Kelly, *If God Already Knows, Why Pray?* (Ross-Shire, Scotland: Christian Focus Publications, 1989).

8. From Rob Goldman, "Healing the Wounds of the World," *The Other Side Magazine,* no. 6 (Nov./Dec. 1991): 24.

9. Helen Adams, *The Christian Year* (Tarrytown, N.Y.: Fleming H. Revell Co. Publishers, 1991), 9–28.

10. Oswald Chambers, *My Utmost for His Highest* (Grand Rapids, Mich.: Discovery House Publishers, 1992), 6–20 and 8–28.

II

When It's All Been Said and Done

Our entire lives are spent with an eye on the future. First we look ahead to the time when we get out from under the restraints of parents and teachers. Then it's marriage, family, and getting our footing on the ladder of success. Finally, we look toward retirement, a chance to kick back and enjoy the good life, whatever we envision that to be. We've all had our share of dreams, expectations, and our *somedays*. But when it comes to looking ahead to the end of our lives, we tend to stop looking ahead. There is a wide range of emotions associated with the inevitable termination of life as we know it. This is the *someday* that few of us want to think about, much less talk about.

Once again I find myself in a situation having to do with the topic that I'm writing about. I have been in this position before, and I know that the Sovereignty of God is our only comfort when dealing with the "iffy" outcome of medical tests.

If the reports are good, we thank God profusely and vow to make good on the promises we made to Him between the time of the tests and the results. But how do we respond to Him when the reports are ominous? How do we deal with the barrage of questions?

Why didn't I take better care of myself?

Why didn't I go to the doctor sooner?

How am I going to get through this?

What do I do first?

Is this it for me?

Am I doing to die?

The answer to the first two questions are of no use to us now, so we must lay those aside. The answers to the last four questions can be found where all the answers to life are found—in the Word of God.

> Do not fret *or* have any anxiety about anything, but in every circumstance and in everything, by prayer *and* petition (definite requests), with thanksgiving, continue to make your wants known to God. And God's peace [shall be yours, *that tranquil state of a soul assured of its salvation through Christ,* and so content with its earthly lot of whatever sort that is, that peace] which transcends all understanding shall garrison *and* mount guard over your hearts and minds in Christ Jesus (Phil. 4:6,7). (Emphasis added)

The tranquil state of a soul assured of its salvation through Christ is what I will remember most about my friend Herbert Hawkins. It was with a frail and failing voice that he prayed the 23rd Psalm for the last time, yet his spirit remained confident. He had hidden this Scripture in his heart, and in the end it was upon these very words that he leaned and found the courage to face and to conquer death. His wife, Betty, gives this account of their last precious moments with his family around him.

> Herb showed our family how to live in health and in illness and taught us how to die with God's grace evident in every way. We will never forget the experience of

being with him and the awesome presence of the Lord as he was released from his earthly body. We waved good-bye through our tears. We had seen death swallowed up in victory.

As Herb's breathing was slowing near the end, it reminded me of the butterfly that has to struggle out of the cocoon in order to bring strength to fly when it is free. When the outer shell falls away, the butterfly spreads its wings and soars into the sky, free to fulfill its new life in a completely different form. Herb has now entered his eternal destiny free to explore the delights of Heaven. He is experiencing the wonderful things God has prepared for those who trust in Him, and he sees face-to-face the One in Whom he has believed all these years. To God be the glory!

Today I visited with my friend Monique Nelson. When she and Joe married 37 years ago, he told her, "We love God and we love each other, and we are going to invest ourselves in others." That they kept covenant with God and each other was evidenced by the 200-plus visitors who filed in and out of Joe's hospital room the last week of his life. At one point in our conversation Monique opened up his Bible, pointed to a passage, and said, "This is why we were so happy." Then she read from Philippians 2:2–4:

If you have any encouragement from being united with Christ, if any comfort from His love, if any fellowship with the Spirit, if any tenderness and compassion, then make my joy complete by being like-minded, having the same love, being one in spirit and purpose. Do nothing out of selfish ambition or vain conceit, but in humility consider others better than yourselves. Each of you should look not only to your own interests, but also to the interests of others. (NIV)

Just before Joe lost consciousness, Monique asked him if he was afraid. He answered her in what would be among his last words. "God has not given me a spirit of fear, but of power and of love and of a sound mind" (2 Tim. 1:7). When the hope of things to come is a living certainty in the life of an individual, not even death can steal the peace that passes all understanding, nor can it quench the expectancy of what lies ahead.

> Eye has not seen and ear has not heard and it has not entered into the heart of man, [all that] God has prepared (made and keeps ready) for those who love Him [who hold Him in affectionate reverence, promptly obeying Him and gratefully recognizing the benefits He has bestowed] (1 Cor: 2:9).

THERE COMES A TIME

There is an old story concerning a young prince who wanted his tutor to give him some instruction about preparing for death. "Plenty of time for that when you are older," was the reply. "No," said the prince, "I have been to the churchyard and measured the graves, and there are many shorter than I am."[1]

We can talk all we want to about the future, but our days are numbered! This doesn't come as any surprise; it's just not something we like to dwell on. Yet it is only when we are prepared for death that we are prepared to get the most out of life now.

In Philippians 3:16 we are instructed to "hold true to what we have already attained and walk and order our lives by that." It is also by holding true to what we have already attained that we are best prepared for death. When our lives are ordered by faith in

Christ, we have learned to rely on Him. What gives us the confidence in our declining years is that once we have yielded ourselves to Him, He takes hold of us and keeps us to the end.

> I will be your God through all your lifetime, yes even when your hair is white with age. I made you and I will care for you. I will carry you along and be your Savior (Isa. 46:4 TLB).

When we have lived in covenant love with God, we can approach the end of our days on earth with the same confidence in which we have lived out our days. "For this God is our God forever and ever; He will be our guide [even] until death" (Ps. 48:14). Remember, the same Power that raised Christ from the dead will attend us when we make our exit. If there is no living soul present with us at the time, the Holy Spirit will be with us. "Precious in the sight of the Lord is the death of His saints (His loving ones)" (Ps. 116:15).

Whenever I learn of a death, the departure of the individual is always secondary. What most concerns me is, *where are they now?* Each day, while thousands are taking off on scheduled flights around the world, there are, as already noted, an average of 145,000 individuals who are taking off *from* the world! And God alone knows how many of them know where *they* are going, or how many had any warning that they were leaving!

SOMETHING IN COMMON

Two men met for the first time at a wedding. Both had climbed to the top of the ladder in their respective professions and shared an interest in golf and investments. Although neither of them knew it at the time, they also held something else in common: inside each of them was the same ticking bomb. Two weeks after the wedding, one learns he has stage-four cancer of the bone. Two years later the other is diagnosed with stage-four cancer of the pancreas.

Four years from the time of their first meeting, these two men continue to have something in common: they are now living in Heaven. But their departures were completely different. Both were raised in the church, yet at the time their cancers were discovered, only one of them was secure in his faith; the other was still searching. But God would work all things—including cancer—for the good of this man's soul to end his search and return him to the faith of his childhood. Thanks be to God for answered prayer. Thanks be to God for so great a salvation.

In the past four years I've seen four individuals (all playing a significant role in my life) pass through the valley of the shadow of death. And in each case it was apparent that God was applying some finishing touches to their lives. I saw new love connections established between family members, a laying aside of the less important for the more important, a new resolve to seek after God for whatever time was left.

I watched as our covenant-keeping God worked through His covenant-keeping people to provide for a covenant-keeping servant to allow her to live out her final days at home rather than in a hospital. And finally, I saw the blinded heart of a woman regain its sight, until what once separated her from her daughter was no longer an issue. Time was short. Loving and forgiving became the issue—the only issue. If any of these individuals had died suddenly, this peacemaking between loved ones and with God would have been impossible. There are advantages to knowing ahead of time that our days are dwindling.

What are we leaving behind? What are we withholding from those who are leaving? Do we have unspoken words of forgiveness for some, of love and appreciation for others? Or do we leave the heartbreaking silence that haunts those who remain?

Pride dies the hardest! Say what you have to say now so you won't have to wrestle with, *If only I had it to do over again.* Remember, both the leaving and the left behind are speechless in the end.

PROMISES, PROMISES

We brought nothing into the world and we can take nothing with us when we leave (1 Tim. 6:7). However, those of us who put our trust in Christ will carry with us the priceless promises of God. The very promises that sustain our Christian walk will, in the end, usher us into His presence.

> I am [Myself] the Resurrection and the Life. Whoever believes in (adheres to, trust in, and relies on) Me, although he may die, yet he shall live (John 11:25).

> In My Father's house there are many dwelling places (homes). If it were not so, I would have told you; for I am going away to prepare a place for you. And when (if) I go and make ready a place for you, I will come back again and will take you to Myself, that where I am you may be also (John 14:2, 3).

The night our Lord appealed to the Father on behalf of His disciples and those of us who would come after them, our place in Heaven was assured, for His prayers for His people were fulfilled in the speaking of them. When it comes to the time of my departure, if I'm unable to do it on my own, I will ask my loved ones to read these words aloud. I can think of no greater comfort for them or for me than to remember that He prayed for us as He prepared to die for us, and because He did, we have nothing to fear at the end of our earthly pilgrimage.

Neither for these alone do I pray [it is not for their sake only that I make this request], but also for all those who will ever come to believe in (trust in, cling to, rely on) Me through their word and teaching (John 17:20).

Father, I desire that they also whom You have entrusted to Me [as Your gift to Me] may be with Me where I am, so that they may see My glory, which You have given Me (Your love gift to Me); for You loved Me before the foundation of the world (John 17:24).

Death is, in the final analysis, the crowning experience of the Christian life, the ultimate healing, the end and the beginning for which we were created. We can commit our spirit to the One Who birthed it, with the assurance of the Heavenly salutation: "Enter into the joy of your Lord" (Matt. 25:21).

It may appear that we are trapped between opposing principles when we consider giving an account of our lives before Christ. Salvation by grace alone lest anyone boast (Eph. 2:9) and faith without works is dead (James 2:26), and now the judgment seat of Christ? (2 Cor. 5:10). The two are reconciled, as Oswald Chambers explains, "If you will learn here and now to live under the scrutiny of Christ's pure light, your final judgment will bring you only delight in seeing the work God has done in you."[2]

Once again we are reminded of God's part and our part. It is only because we are His handiwork that we can expect to hear, *well done, good and faithful servant* (Matt. 25:21). Covenant is lived out daily, often moment by moment, and there will never be a time, this side of Heaven, when we won't have to vote down some aspect of our human nature in favor of the new nature the Holy Spirit is refining in us.

It will be the fruit of our service and our motives for serving that Christ will judge. Every family is a mission field, as is every neighborhood and every workplace. It won't be how much talent we had, but how we used it; not how much money, but how we spent it; not how much time or how much influence, but that we gave graciously to God and His Kingdom. God gives more than enough to invest, and when we spend His provisions wisely, He will replenish so we can invest again. We are eternal beings. The best investment we can make is in eternity!

I've just learned that the danger lurking in the first set of medical tests, mentioned at the beginning of this chapter, turned out to be something other than what was first suspected. Once again my time has been extended, and I can honestly say that I am grateful for the wake-up call this experience has given me. Don't think for a moment that what I've been saying to you I don't continually say to myself, for what matters most to me is that I live out my life in a manner worthy of my Lord and Savior.

> We glide along the tides of time as swiftly as a racing river, and vanish as quickly as a dream . . . Teach us to number our days and to recognize how few they are; help us to spend them as we should (Ps. 90:5,12 TLB).

Now that I'm a member of the over-55 group, the greater portion of my journey is behind me. I've gone from the tiny sailboat in the painting at the foot of my hospital bed when I was 40 to a much larger vessel. There is no question as to the strength of *this* boat, for it is designed and powered by my Lord and the covenant love we have for each other. Whether the last few miles of my voyage will find me in choppy waters or whether I glide smoothly into the dock, like you, I have no way of knowing. But I do know that there is a place waiting for me when I get there.

And I can thank God that my days are numbered. It is not death that breathes down my neck, but the sweet breath of His promise of new life, closer now than ever before. I feel it in the stiffness of the morning, in the slowing of pace, in the tenderness of my back, and in the time it takes to do less than I used to do with twice the effort. Yet I can rejoice in the dwindling number of my days. For soon my Savior comes for me. And I can say, "Come quickly, Lord Jesus," and know I do not betray my heart.

Until then, I have promises to keep.
And so do you.

Notes

1. Joseph S. Exell, *The Biblical Illustrator,* John Vol. 2, Ch. 9, Baker Books, 1977, 127.
2. Oswald Chambers, *My Utmost for His Highest,* (Grand Rapids, Mich.: Discovery House, 1992), 3–16.

Then those who feared the Lord talked often one to another; and the Lord listened and heard it, and a book of remembrance was written before Him of those who reverenced and worshipfully feared the Lord *and* who thought on His name. And they shall be Mine, says the Lord of Hosts, in that day when I publicly recognize *and* openly declare them to be My jewels (My special possession, My peculiar treasure). And I will spare them, as a man who spares his own son who serves him (Mal. 3:16-17).